pitman 2000 SHORTHAND

FIRST COURSE

D0334378

pitman 2000 SHORTHAND
FIRST COURSE

Pitman Publishing

First published 1975
Reprinted 1975 (*with amendments*)
Reprinted 1976 (*twice*)

PITMAN PUBLISHING LTD
Pitman House, 39 Parker Street, London WC2B 5PB, UK

PITMAN PUBLISHING CORPORATION
FEARON PUBLISHERS INC
6 Davis Drive, Belmont, California 94002, USA

PITMAN PUBLISHING PTY LTD
Pitman House, 158 Bouverie Street, Carlton, Victoria 3053,
Australia

PITMAN PUBLISHING
COPP CLARK PUBLISHING
517 Wellington Street West, Toronto M5V 1G1, Canada

SIR ISAAC PITMAN LTD
Banda Street, PO Box 46038, Nairobi, Kenya, East Africa

PITMAN PUBLISHING CO SA (PTY) LTD
Craighall Mews, Jan Smuts Avenue, Craighall Park,
Johannesburg 2001, South Africa

Isaac Pitman

© Sir Isaac Pitman and Sons Ltd 1975

All Rights Reserved. This edition of Sir Isaac Pitman's
system of shorthand is the exclusive copyright of
Sir Isaac Pitman & Sons Ltd. No part of this publication
may be reproduced, stored in a retrieval system, or transmitted,
in any form or by any means, electronic, mechanical,
photocopying, recording and/or otherwise, without
the prior written permission of the publishers.

ISBN: 0 273 00883 8

Text set in 10/11 pt Monotype Baskerville, printed by photolithography,
and bound in Great Britain at The Pitman Press, Bath

G6—(S.2000:26)

PREFACE

'Pitman 2000' is a shorthand specification developed by the Pitman Group. Although it is a technical modification of Pitman New Era, which is the most widely used international system today, it cannot be too strongly emphasized that both Pitman 2000 and Pitman New Era are professional shorthand systems and are both Pitmans Shorthand.

Pitman 2000 Shorthand represents spoken sounds by written signs. Writing by sound means writing words as they are pronounced and not according to longhand spelling. The following illustration shows how to think of words when writing shorthand:

palm	is	p-ah-m	wrought	is	r-aw-t
pale	is	p-ay-l	coal	is	k-oh-l
key	is	k-ee	tomb	is	t-oo-m

Look at the words again, and their corresponding pronunciation, and note that:

(a) just as the spelling of words is made up of consonants and vowels, so too is their pronunciation;
(b) silent letters are not represented in the pronunciation, e.g., tomb, palm;
(c) generally speaking, there are fewer letters used to represent the pronunciation of words than the spelling, e.g., r-aw-t (wrought).

In longhand the alphabet consists of consonants and vowels, combinations of which are used to form words. In shorthand special signs are used to represent only those consonants and vowels which are actually sounded when pronouncing words. The shorthand alphabet therefore consists of strokes which represent the consonant sounds, and dots and dashes which represent the vowel sounds.

Any consonant symbol or combination of consonant symbols, with

v

or without vowel signs, is known as an outline. Having written an outline correctly, a writer of Pitman 2000 Shorthand is able to recognize it and transcribe it without any hesitation.

Pitman 2000 Shorthand is designed for quick and therefore easy learning with a realistic speed potential to meet the demands of the business and industrial world. The outlines can be written swiftly and the writer is able to transcribe them quickly and accurately into typewritten or handwritten form.

The Aims of this Book are:

to present the complete theory of Pitman 2000 Shorthand in clear and easy stages;

to give adequate theory practice within a working vocabulary; and

to introduce transcription training and speed development.

The Aims of the Learner should be:

to understand every shorthand rule in each unit thoroughly and to follow the suggested practice plans;

to be able to read, write, recognize and remember each outline without any hesitation; and

to read and write some shorthand every day.

How to Use This Book

Work through each unit thoroughly and conscientiously. No two students learn in exactly the same way or in the same amount of time and the practice plans may be adjusted to meet individual needs. It is essential to use the book in the order in which the units are presented and to learn and understand each shorthand rule before proceeding to the next unit.

Short Forms and Phrases

Short forms are the signs for some of the most frequently used words in the English language. It is most unlikely that any statement on a general business or industrial subject could be written in shorthand without using at least one short form, and therefore all short forms should be learned so thoroughly that they are written accurately and without hesitation, and read back easily. Phrases in Pitman 2000 Shorthand are outlines formed together for groups of words which are used frequently, and the principles of phrasing must be understood so that they can be used whenever necessary. Short forms and phrases are positive speed builders.

Reading Practice

The aim of every shorthand student is to write the spoken word at speed and to transcribe notes accurately and quickly. The development of the shorthand skill is positively aided when some part of every day is devoted to the reading of shorthand. Each exercise should be read, referring to the key whenever necessary, in preparation for copying and dictation practice. Any outline which causes hesitation in the first reading should be practised until it is completely familiar so that a second and third reading of any exercise will be at considerably higher speeds. Each shorthand exercise should be read as quickly as longhand. In addition to reading printed shorthand, time should be devoted each day to improving the speed of reading from your own notes. The whole purpose of taking shorthand notes is to be able to transcribe accurately and at speed. The monthly magazine *2000* provides excellent additional shorthand material for reading and copying practice.

Dictation Practice

After reading through and preparing each exercise, it is essential to practise writing it from dictation. Students who are teaching them-selves Pitman 2000 should try to persuade someone to read to them each day from the longhand keys, or should use recorded dictation. The shorthand notes should be transcribed by reading back to the dictator and then by writing or typing them. Shorthand notes should be checked against the printed outlines in the book, errors or omissions corrected, and the correct outlines practised. The next time those words are dictated the outlines will be written correctly and without hesitation. Each rule should be thoroughly learned as it is introduced. Correct shorthand outlines are easier to read and faster to write. Attention should always be paid to the length of the strokes, the position of each outline in relation to the writing line, and the placing of the essential vowel signs.

The Longhand Keys

Each Reading and Writing Practice has a longhand key, usually on the facing page of the book, and this should be referred to if necessary, when reading the shorthand for the first time. If the key is referred to it should be understood why the shorthand outlines are written that way and the outlines should then be practised. The next practice should not be read until the previous one can be read without reference to the key. The word count which is given in brackets at the end of each sentence and continuous passage will help dictators to calculate the dictation speed.

Speed

After a thorough preparation of each exercise, the aim should be to write it from dictation as fast as possible. The reading speed of prepared material is higher than the present writing speed. After the completion of the study of Pitman 2000, followed by a course of revision and speed development, it will be possible to attain a writing speed of 140 w.p.m.

Homework

Practising shorthand daily will ensure steady progress in the skill. A student of Pitman 2000 Shorthand should expect to spend some part of every day reading, practising outlines, learning short forms and phrasing principles and preparing the exercise material to be used the following day.

Posture

Cultivating a good posture is important; not only does it suggest alertness and efficiency but it promotes a better writing style and actually prevents fatigue. Feet should be kept firmly on the floor, the back well supported by the chair, and the weight of the upper part of the body on the non-writing arm.

Writing Materials

Use a good fountain-pen with a fine flexible nib, and a notebook of good-quality paper with a spiral binding at the top so that the paper lies flat. Good writing materials help the writer of Pitman 2000 Shorthand to write and then read the outlines more easily.

Additional Practice Material

Whilst studying this book it will be helpful to use, at the same time, the specially prepared and graded material provided in *Pitman 2000 First Course Facility Drills*, and *Pitman 2000 Dictation Practice* and its complementary *Workbook*, *Parts 1 and 2* with the related tapes or cassettes. In any skill, constant practice makes perfect, and by using these additional materials a greater efficiency will be achieved in a shorter time.

After First Course

On completion of this *First Course*, a good knowledge of Pitman 2000 Shorthand will have been attained. A complete theory revision and vocabulary extension is then necessary in preparation for a secretarial post. *Pitman 2000 Shorthand: First Course Review* provides a full theory revision, with many additional examples of the rules of the system, a vocabulary range of five thousand words, and some concentrated revision material. *Pitman 2000 Shorthand : Skill Book* is designed to increase the reading and writing skills in Pitman 2000 Shorthand by a full understanding of the phrasing principles which are explained and illustrated. Read all the Pitman 2000 Shorthand provided in *2000* magazine each month to complete a satisfactory programme of revision work.

ACKNOWLEDGEMENT

The publishers wish to thank Mr Bryan Coombs for his assistance with this book, which has drawn upon his unique experiences as an international court reporter, as a lecturer on the staff of a college of education and as a teacher in further education.

This book has been adopted by Pitmans Correspondence College as part of the Home Study Course Pitman 2000 Shorthand for Beginners.

For further details of this course, please contact: Pitmans Correspondence College (Dept. PP), Worcester Road, Wimbledon, SW19 7QQ, England (tel: (01) 947-6993).

CONTENTS

Welcome to Pitman 2000, but have you read the Preface

UNIT 1
P, B, T, D
Vowels Ā and Ō
Circle S

P is a thin stroke written **downwards** .

Vowel Ā is a heavy dot. It is always written at the middle of a stroke, and is always added after the writing of the stroke has been completed. In the word **pay** the vowel is sounded **after** the P and is placed **after** the stroke P (on the right-hand side).

In the word **ape** the vowel Ā is sounded **before** the P and is placed **before** the stroke P (on the left-hand side) **after** the stroke has been written.

B is a thick stroke written **downwards** .

Vowel Ō is a heavy dash. It is always written at the middle of a stroke, and is added **after** the writing of the stroke has been completed. In the word **oboe** the vowels are sounded **before** and **after** the B and are placed **before** and **after** the stroke B (on the left- and right-hand sides).

T is a thin stroke written **downwards** . In the word **oat** the vowel is sounded **before** the T and is placed **before** the stroke T (on the left-hand side).

D is a thick stroke written **downwards** . A small circle written as shown at the **end** of the stroke adds the sound of S or Z . In the words **days/daze** the vowel is sounded **after** the D and is placed **after** the stroke D (on the right-hand side).

The sound of S at the beginning of a word is shown by a small circle written on the right-hand side of straight downstrokes:

stay (sounded first)

days/daze (sounded last)

stays (sounded first and last)

Always complete the writing of strokes **before** adding the vowels

---

POSITION WRITING

In the following examples all the single downstrokes are written to the line.

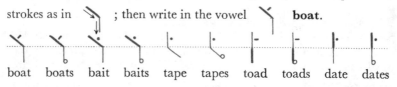

ape apes pay pays soap soaps pose space stow stows oboe oboes

stay stays oat oats toe/tow toes/tows aid aids day days

Practise writing these outlines in your notebook. Write each outline several times, repeating the words out loud as you write. When two or more strokes are joined together the first stroke is written to the line and the outline is completed without lifting the pen. Complete the strokes as in ⟍ ; then write in the vowel ⟍ **boat.**

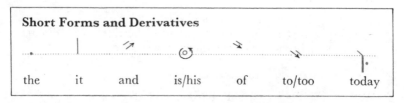

boat boats bait baits tape tapes toad toads date dates

Write each outline several times, repeating the word aloud as you write.

SHORT FORMS AND DERIVATIVES

Certain words are used so frequently in our language that special signs called short forms are used to represent them.

Derivative is the term for a word built from another word called the root word.

Short Forms and Derivatives

the	it	and	is/his	of	to/too	today

Practise these short forms until they are completely familiar.

PHRASES

The outlines for two or more words may be joined without lifting the pen, to make outlines called phrases. Good phrasing leads to high-speed writing. Phrasing is used, however, only when outlines join naturally and can be read back easily.

In phrases the word **the** is represented by a tick, written upwards or downwards to form a sharp angle.

The first word in a phrase is written in its usual position.

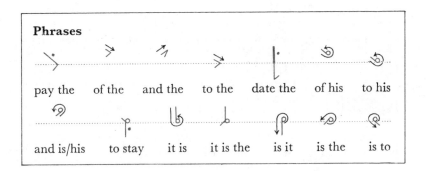

pay the	of the	and the	to the	date the	of his	to his
and is/his	to stay	it is	it is the	is it	is the	is to

PUNCTUATION, ETC.

This is the same in shorthand as in longhand except for:

full stop   question mark   exclamation mark

dash   hyphen   parentheses

PRACTICE PLAN

1. Read through the exercise, referring to the key if necessary.
2. Practise writing any outline which caused any hesitancy in the reading. Say the word to yourself as you write.
3. Read through the exercise again, aiming for fluency in your reading.
4. Write each sentence until you can write it easily and rapidly.
5. Write each sentence from dictation. Keep your book open for reference if necessary.
6. Read the sentences from your own shorthand notes.

READING AND WRITING PRACTICE

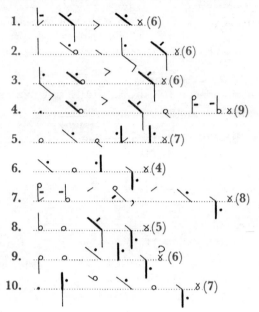

1. .... x (6)
2. .... x (6)
3. .... x (6)
4. .... x (9)
5. .... x (7)
6. .... x (4)
7. .... x (8)
8. .... x (5)
9. .... x (6)
10. .... x (7)

Key to Reading and Writing Practice

1. Tow the boat to the bay. (**6**)
2. It pays to tape the boat. (**6**)
3. Tape the base of the boat. (**6**)
4. The base of the boat is to stow oats. (**9**)
5. His pay is to aid the day. (**7**)
6. Pay his aid today. (**4**)
7. Stow the oats and soap, and pay today. (**8**)
8. It is his boat today. (**5**)
9. Is it his pay day today? (**6**)
10. The date of his pay is today. (**7**)

UNIT 2
K, G, M, N, NG
Dot ING

The strokes for **K**, **G**, **M**, **N** and **NG** are horizontal, and are written from **left to right**:

K (thin) → **G** (thick) → **M** (thin and curved) ⌒

N (thin and curved) ⌣ **NG** (thick and curved) ⌣

If a vowel is sounded first it is added **above** these strokes, and written **below** if it is sounded after. Always write the stroke first.

ache	may	aim	no	gay	oak	go	own

Read the outlines and then write them several times.

POSITION WRITING

In the following examples all single horizontal strokes are written on the line. When horizontal strokes are combined with other strokes the first downstroke is written to the line.

DOT ING

A dot at the end of an outline represents the suffix **ING**.
Always write the **circle S** on top of horizontal strokes and inside curved strokes:

ache	aches	aching	cope	copes	coping	go	goes	going

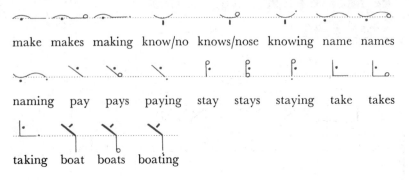

make makes making know/no knows/nose knowing name names

naming pay pays paying stay stays staying take takes

taking boat boats boating

Read the outlines and then write them several times.

Short Forms and Derivatives

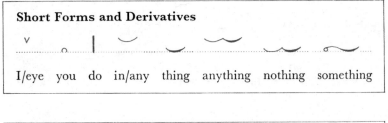

I/eye you do in/any thing anything nothing something

Phrases

I do do you in the in any and I you may I know the

in his to go

PRACTICE PLAN

1. Read through the exercise, referring to the key if necessary.
2. Practise writing any outline which caused any hesitancy in the reading. Say the word to yourself as you write.
3. Read through the exercise again, aiming for fluency in your reading.
4. Write each sentence until you can write it easily and rapidly.
5. Write each sentence from dictation. Keep your book open for reference if necessary.
6. Read the sentences from your own shorthand notes.

UNIT 2

READING AND WRITING PRACTICE

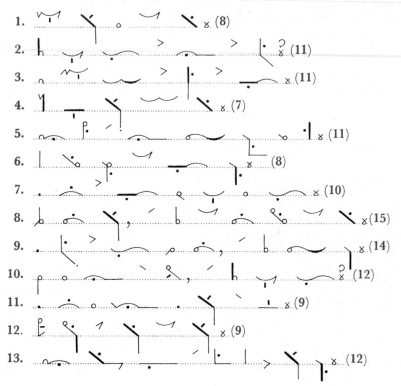

Key to Reading and Writing Practice

1. I know the boat is in the bay. **(8)**
2. Do you know the name of the make of the tape? **(11)**
3. You and I know nothing of the date of the game. **(11)**
4. I do go boating in any bay. **(7)**
5. You may stay and make something to take to his aid. **(11)**
6. It pays to stay in the game today. **(8)**
7. The aim of the game is to know his name. **(10)**
8. It is the same boat, and it is in the same space in the bay. **(15)**
9. The taping of the name is the same, and it is something to do. **(14)**
10. Is it his make of soap, and do you know the name? **(12)**
11. The aim is to make the boat of oak. **(9)**
12. Stow the spade and the bait in the boat. **(9)**
13. You may bake the cake and take it to the boat today. **(12)**

UNIT 3
F, V, Th, TH
SES, SEZ, ZES, ZEZ
Vowels Ĕ and Ŭ

F is a thin, curved downstroke ⟍ :

foe   face   fade   fake   folk   safe

V is a thick, curved downstroke ⟍ :

save   vote   vogue   vague   mauve

Th (as in **faith**) is a thin, curved downstroke ⟨⟨ :

oath   faith   both

TH (as in **th**ey) is a thick, curved downstroke ⟨⟨ :

they   bathe   though

Read the outlines and then practise writing them several times.

The sound of **SES, SEZ, ZES** or **ZEZ** is represented by a large circle written at the end of an outline:

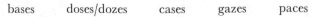

bases   doses/dozes   cases   gazes   paces

Make sure this **SES** circle is written larger than the **circle S**:

dose/doze doses/dozes dosing/dozing gaze gazes gazing

space spaces spacing base bases basing pace paces pacing

case cases casing

Read the outlines and then write them several times.

The **S, SES, SEZ, ZES,** and **ZEZ** circles are **always** written inside curved strokes:

save saves face faces nose noses bathes safes

The short sound **Ĕ** (as in **bet**) is represented by a light dot which is always placed at the middle of a stroke, either before or after it:

bet bets betting egg eggs egging guess guesses guessing

beg begs begging deck decks decking set sets setting

sense senses sensing them debt debts excess

Read the outlines and then write them several times.

The short sound Ŭ (as in **up**) is represented by a light dash which is always placed at the middle of a stroke, either before or after it:

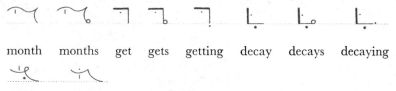

up   pub   pubs   tub   tubs   does   come   comes   coming   success

gum   gums   sum   sums   summing   sun/son   suns/sons   sunning

Read the outlines and then write them several times.

POSITION WRITING

When an outline begins with a horizontal stroke and is followed by a downstroke, it is the downstroke which **positions** the outline. Write in all the vowel signs **after** the outline has been completed:

month   months   get   gets   getting   decay   decays   decaying

unsafe   enough

Read the outlines and then write them several times.

The **circle S** is always written **outside** the angle made by two straight strokes:

custom   customs   desk   dusk   tusk

Read the outlines and then write them several times.

Two light dashes under an outline (written **upwards**) indicate a word requiring an initial capital letter:

Sunday   Monday   May   Dunmow   Exmouth   Kay

Short Forms and Derivatives

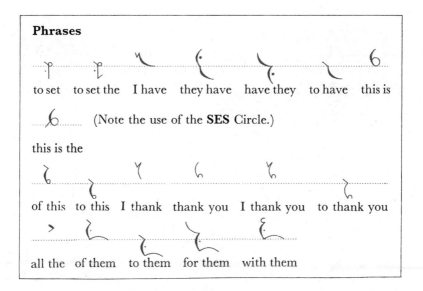

for   have   be   being   this   all   thank   thanks   thanking   a/an

with

Phrases

to set   to set the   I have   they have   have they   to have   this is

(Note the use of the **SES** Circle.)

this is the

of this   to this   I thank   thank you   I thank you   to thank you

all the   of them   to them   for them   with them

PRACTICE PLAN

1. Read through the exercise, referring to the key if necessary.
2. Practise writing any outline which caused any hesitancy in the reading. Say the word to yourself as you write.
3. Read through the exercise again, aiming for fluency in your reading.
4. Write each sentence until you can write it easily and rapidly.
5. Write each sentence from dictation. Keep your book open for reference if necessary.
6. Read the sentences from your own shorthand notes.

READING AND WRITING PRACTICE

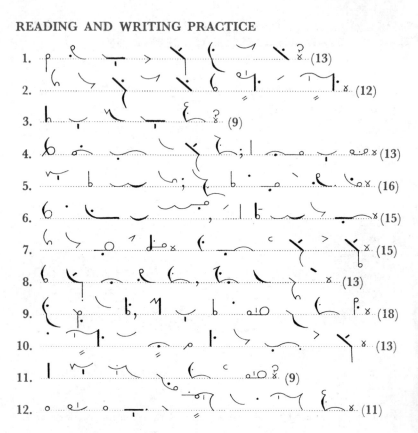

1. (13)
2. (12)
3. (9)
4. (13)
5. (16)
6. (15)
7. (15)
8. (13)
9. (18)
10. (13)
11. (9)
12. (11)

Key to Reading and Writing Practice

1. Is it safe to go to the boat they have in the bay? (**13**)
2. Thank you for the bathe in the bay this Sunday and Monday. (**12**)
3. Do you know I have to go with them? (**9**)
4. This is the same name for both of them; it makes no sense. (**13**)
5. I know it is nothing for you; for them it is a case of saving face. (**16**)
6. This is a vague thing in any case, and it does nothing for the game. (**15**)
7. Thank you for the cases and the desks. They came with both of the boats. (**15**)
8. This voting may save them, and they may have to thank you all. (**13**)
9. They have to stay for days, and I do know it is a success to have them stay. (**18**)
10. A Monday in May is the day for the naming of the boat. (**13**)
11. Do I know enough to face them with success? (**9**)
12. His son is going to Exmouth for a month with them. (**11**)

UNIT 4
L, W, Y
Past-tense sounds T and D

L is a thin curved upstroke _____ :

low   load   loads   loading   lay   lays   laying   less   else   sail   sails

sailing   coal   coals   sell   sells   selling   slow   sleigh/slay

sleighs/slays   delay   delays   delaying   lake   lakes   leg   legs   length

lengths   lung   lungs   develop   develops   developing

Read the **circle S** first, in the middle, or last, wherever it is written. Write the circle inside the first curved stroke.

lesson   lessons   muscle/mussel   muscles/mussels

Read the outlines and then write them several times.

14

W is a thin straight upstroke with a small hook at the beginning :

way/weigh   ways/weighs   weighing   Wednesday   well

wake   wakes   waking   woke   wed   wedding

Circle S is written inside the hook of **W** to represent the sound of

SW :

sway   sways   swaying   swell   swells   swelling

Read the outlines and then write them several times.

The sound added to most verbs to make the past tense is either that of a **T** or a **D**. These past tenses are shown by writing a disjoined stroke **T** or **D** (according to whichever is sounded) close to the root outline:

pay paid unpaid delay delayed face faced name named

weigh   weighed   sway   swayed   daze   dazed   developed

Read the outlines and then write them several times.

Y is a thin straight upstroke with a small hook at the beginning

yellow   young   yolk/yoke   yes

Read the outlines and then write them several times.

Short Forms and Derivatives

as/has   but   will   we   yesterday   thanked

Phrases

In phrasing, use only the first half of the short form **I** before the stroke **L**.

I will   I will be the   you will   you will be the   it will

it will be the   I thanked   they will   they will be the

you will have   you will have the   but the   but you

but you will be the   we have   we have the   we will

we will be the   and as/has   as/has the   is as   as is

Note that the outline for **but the** is tilted to the right to give a better angle.

To form a phrase, **tick the** can be added to a disjoined **T** or **D**.

paid the   named the   weighed the   developed the

PRACTICE PLAN

1. Read through the exercise, referring to the key if necessary.
2. Practise writing any outline which caused any hesitancy in the reading. Say the word to yourself as you write.
3. Read through the exercise again, aiming for fluency in your reading.
4. Write each sentence until you can write it easily and rapidly.
5. Write each sentence from dictation. Keep your book open for reference if necessary.
6. Read the sentences from your own shorthand notes.

READING AND WRITING PRACTICE

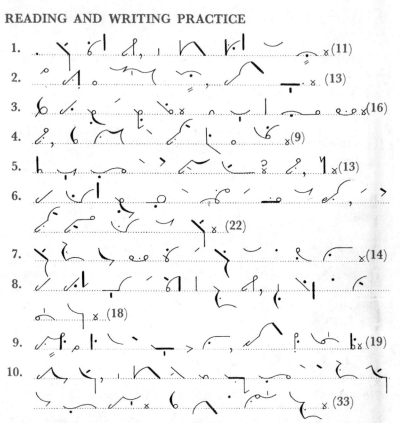

Key to Reading and Writing Practice

1. The boat sailed yesterday, but it will be delayed in May. **(11)**
2. As the wedding is in the month of May, we will be going. **(13)**
3. This is the way to save and to stay the pace. You know it makes sense. **(16)**
4. Yes, this length of yellow tape is for sale. **(9)**
5. Do you know the names of all the young folk? Yes, I do. **(13)**
6. We failed to save the cases of mussels and eggs in the swell, and all the yellow yolks fell in the boat. **(22)**
7. Both of them have the sense to sail and bathe in a safe lake. **(14)**
8. We weighed the coal and sold it to them yesterday, but they paid a low sum for it. **(18)**
9. Wednesday is the day for all to go to the lake, and we will be staying for some days. **(19)**
10. We have the vote, but it will be up to you to get the names of all of them and vote for the name we know. This will be a lesson for them. **(33)**

UNIT 5

Upward and downward R

R is a thin stroke. It may be written upwards as a straight stroke

or downwards as a curved stroke.

Upward **R** is used when the sound of **R** begins a word. Write circles **S** or **SES** on top of upward **R**:

ray   rays/raise   raises   raising   rope   ropes   roping   roped

road   roads   railway   railways   rose/rows   roses

rung   rungs   red

Upward **R** is used in the **middle** of an outline:

purpose   purposes   forth   board   boards   boarded   boarding

bird   birds   work   works   working   worked   girl   girls

Upward **R** is used at the end of an outline when the **R** is followed by a sounded vowel:

thorough   furrow   burrow

Read the outlines and then write them several times.

Downward **R** is used when a vowel sound **begins** a word and **R** is the
first consonant sound:

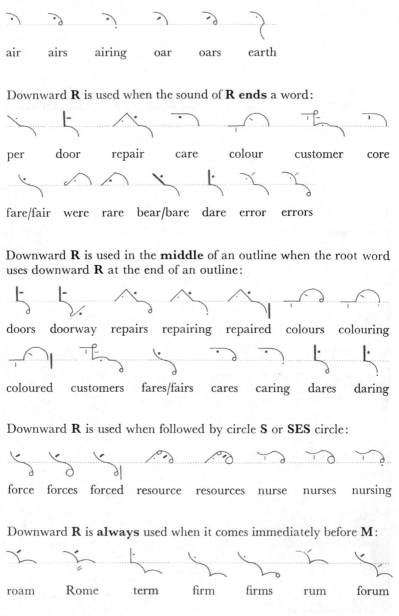

air   airs   airing   oar   oars   earth

Downward **R** is used when the sound of **R ends** a word:

per   door   repair   care   colour   customer   core

fare/fair   were   rare   bear/bare   dare   error   errors

Downward **R** is used in the **middle** of an outline when the root word
uses downward **R** at the end of an outline:

doors   doorway   repairs   repairing   repaired   colours   colouring

coloured   customers   fares/fairs   cares   caring   dares   daring

Downward **R** is used when followed by circle **S** or **SES** circle:

force   forces   forced   resource   resources   nurse   nurses   nursing

Downward **R** is **always** used when it comes immediately before **M**:

roam   Rome   term   firm   firms   rum   forum

Read the outlines and then write them several times.

Short Forms and Derivatives

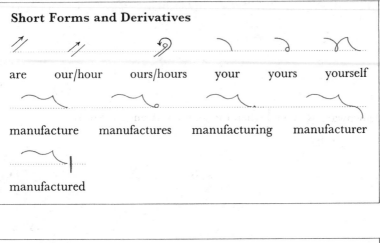

are   our/hour   ours/hours   your   yours   yourself

manufacture   manufactures   manufacturing   manufacturer

manufactured

Phrases

you are   we are   they are   of your   to your   in your   to our   of our

Note that in phrases the **circle S** is used for **us** and **his**:

to us   for us   of us   with us   to his   for his   of his   with his

In some phrases **you** is turned sideways to give an easier joining:

and you   will you   with you

PRACTICE PLAN

1. Read through the exercise, referring to the key if necessary.
2. Practise writing any outline which caused any hesitancy in the reading. Say the word to yourself as you write.
3. Read through the exercise again, aiming for fluency in your reading.
4. Write each sentence until you can write it easily and rapidly.
5. Write each sentence from dictation. Keep your book open for reference if necessary.
6. Read the sentences from your own shorthand notes.

READING AND WRITING PRACTICE

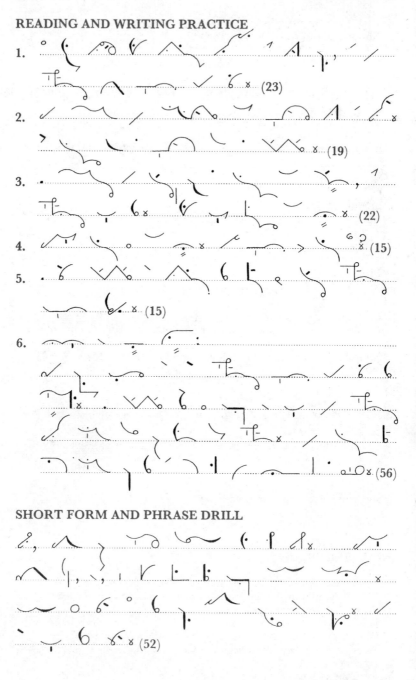

1. ... (23)

2. ... (19)

3. ... (22)

4. ... (15)

5. ... (15)

6. ... (56)

SHORT FORM AND PHRASE DRILL

... (52)

UNIT 5

Key to Reading and Writing Practice

1. As they have the resources they will repair the railway and the road today, and our customers will be coming to our sale. (**23**)

2. We manufacture our envelopes in the colours red and yellow. All the firms have a colour for a purpose. (**19**)

3. The manufacturers are forced to have a firm in Rome, and the customers know this. They will know the terms in May. (**22**)

4. We know the fair is in May. Are you coming to the fair with us? (**15**)

5. The sole purpose of repairing this door is to force customers to come this way. (**15**)

6. Memo to Kay Lake:
   You are to take the names of all customers coming to our sale this Monday. The purpose of this is to get to know our customers well enough for us to thank them for the custom. Our firm does care enough to do this and your aid will make it a success. (**56**)

Key to Short Form and Phrase Drill

Yes, we have to thank the nurses for something they said yesterday. We know you will be thanked, too, but it will take days to get anything in the mail. Nothing is as slow as this today and we have to face up to delays. We all know this is too slow. (**52**)

UNIT 6
Half-length strokes

Strokes may be written half length to indicate a following sound of
T or **D**.

In one-syllable words thin strokes are halved in length to indicate the
following sound of **T**:

coat   coats   coated   cut   cuts   cutting   kept   left   met   pet   pets

late   note   notes   noting   noted   weight/wait   weights/waits

weighting/waiting   weighted/waited   yet   port   ports

Read the outlines and then write them several times.

In one-syllable words thick strokes are halved in length to indicate the
following sound of **D**:

bed   beds   bedding   dead   dud   goad   goaded

Read the outlines and then write them several times.

In words of two or more syllables a stroke is generally halved to indicate
a following sound of **T** or **D**:

deduct   deducts   deducting   deducted   expect   expects   expecting

expected   method   methods   except   excepting   result   results   resulting

resulted   remote   debate   debates   debating   debated

Read the outlines and then write them several times.

Strokes are **not** halved if the halving would not clearly show:

effect   effects   effecting   effected   select   selects   selecting

selected   locate   locates   locating   located

When upward **R** is the first stroke in any outline, it is **not** halved for
T or **D**:

rate   rated   rating   wrote/rote   rut   ruts   roadway

In words of two or more syllables upward **R** is halved for **T** or **D** when
following another stroke, as in:

expert   experts   export   exports   exporting   exported

support supports supporting supported report reports reporting reported

Read the outlines and then write them several times.

The strokes **R** and **L** are not halved for **D** at the end of an outline if a vowel comes between **R-D, L-D**:

railroad   erode   payload

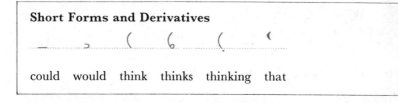

Short Forms and Derivatives

could   would   think   thinks   thinking   that

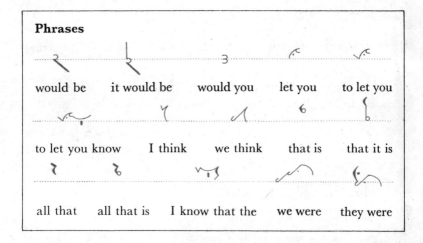

Phrases

would be   it would be   would you   let you   to let you

to let you know   I think   we think   that is   that it is

all that   all that is   I know that the   we were   they were

---

PRACTICE PLAN

1. Read through the exercise, referring to the key if necessary.
2. Practise writing any outline which caused any hesitancy in the reading. Say the word to yourself as you write.
3. Read through the exercise again, aiming for fluency in your reading.
4. Write each sentence until you can write it easily and rapidly.
5. Write each sentence from dictation. Keep your book open for reference if necessary.
6. Read the sentences from your own shorthand notes.

READING AND WRITING PRACTICE

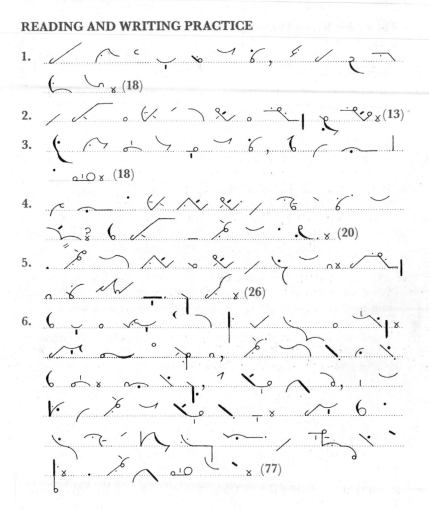

1. (18)

2. (13)

3. (18)

4. (20)

5. (26)

6. (77)

SHORT FORM AND PHRASE DRILL

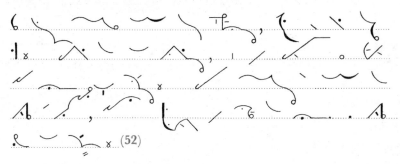

(52)

Key to Reading and Writing Practice

1. We are left with no beds in the sale, and yet we would have kept them for you. (**18**)

2. Our work is thorough and your support is expected to save the exports. (**13**)

3. They have left the sum for the coats in the sale, and this will make it a success. (**18**)

4. Will you make a thorough report supporting our methods of selling in Rome? This work could result in a saving. (**20**)

5. The results in your report to us support our faith in you. We expected you to sell and we think you are going to do well. (**26**)

6. This note is to let you know that your debt to our firm is unpaid. We know that something has upset you, resulting in your being late paying this sum. You may pay today, and the bonus will be yours, but any delay will result in the bonus being cut. We know this is a fair method and it will have the effect of making our customers pay all debts. The result will be success for all. (**77**)

Key to Short Form and Phrase Drill

This firm manufactures anything for your customers, and they have to pay for this aid. We pay for any repairs, but our work is thorough and we make no errors. We are manufacturers of anything for roads and railways, and we may develop our methods for making the roads safe in Rome. (**52**)

UNIT 7
CH, J, SH, S

CH is a thin downstroke :

check   checks   checking   checked   such   much   fetch   fetches

fetching   fetched   touch   touches   touching   touched

Read the outlines and then write them several times.

J is a thick downstroke :

age   ages   ageing   aged   judge   judges   judging   judged   jumbo

jet   jets   jetting   jetted   edge   edges   edging   edged

change   changing   changed   exchange   exchanging   exchanged

page   pages   paging   paged   budget   budgets   budgeting   budgeted

Read the outlines and then write them several times.

SH is a thin curved downstroke ⟋⟍ :

show   shows   showing   showed   shade   shades   shading   shaded

shape   shapes   shaping   shaped   shave   shaves   shaving   shaved

rush   rushes   rushing   rushed

Read the outlines and then write them several times.

S is a thin curved downstroke ⟍ . When **S** is the only consonant sound in a word use stroke **S:**

us   so/sew/sow   sewing/sowing   say   saying   essay

Stroke **S** is also used when a vowel is sounded **before S** at the beginning of a word, or when a vowel **follows S** at the end of a word:

escape   escapes   escaping   escaped   estate   estates   peso

Read the outlines and then write them several times.

Short Forms

shall   which   on   had/dollar   large

Phrases

I shall	I shall be	we shall	we shall be	we shall have	I had

which you which is/which has which are which will which will be

on the

Note that the outline for **on the** is tilted to the right to give a better angle.

PRACTICE PLAN

1. Read through the exercise on the next page, referring to the key if necessary.
2. Practise writing any outline which caused any hesitancy in reading.
3. Write each sentence until you can write it easily and rapidly.
4. Write each sentence from dictation.
5. Read the sentences from your own shorthand notes.
6. Transcribe (by hand, until you can type) the exercise from the textbook as a homework assignment.

READING AND WRITING PRACTICE

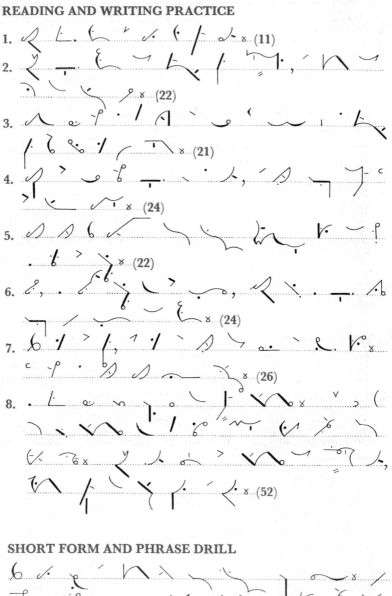

SHORT FORM AND PHRASE DRILL

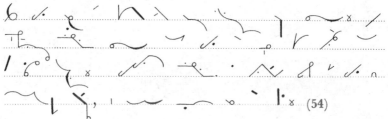

UNIT 7

1. We shall be checking them on the way they judge shows. (**11**)

2. I shall be going with them in the jumbo jet on Monday, and it will be in the air for four hours. (**22**)

3. We have sent such a large load of things that nothing but a jumbo jet of this space age will cope. (**21**)

4. We shall do all the things such as going to a show, and rushing to get in touch with all the folk we know. (**24**)

5. We shall rush this work for your firm so that you will have no delay in setting the edges of the pages. (**22**)

6. Yes, the yellow pages have all the names, and we shall be paying the going rates to get our name in with them. (**24**)

7. This is the age of the jets, and the age of rushing for the sake of saving delays. With such a rush we shall make errors. (**26**)

8. The cheque sent to you today is for Dutch bulbs. I would think your bedding bulbs have large sales and I know they are the result of your thorough methods. I shall be showing some of the bulbs in the Exmouth show, and they will be judged for both shade and shape. (**52**)

Key to Short Form and Phrase Drill

This is the way to save and it will be up to your firm to do something. Our customers expect something in the way of cuts which will result in large sales for them. We were expecting a report yesterday on the way you manufactured the boats, but nothing came to us all day. (**54**)

UNIT 8
Position writing
First-place vowels
(AH, Ă, AW, Ŏ)

In the first seven units, downstrokes and upstrokes have been written downwards **to** the line and upwards **from** the line. This is called the **second position.** In the following examples the first downstroke or upstroke is written **above** the line. This is called the **first position.** First-position single horizontal strokes are written **above** the line.

The long sound of **AH** (as in **car**) is represented by a heavy dot. This dot is placed at the **beginning** of a stroke, either before or after it:

arm   arms   arming   part   parts   parting   guard   March   dark

arch   car   cars   far   farm   farms   farming   farmed   farmer

mark   marks   marking   marked   market   markets   marketing

pass   passes   passing   passed   laugh   regard   regarded

Remember that the **first** vowel sound in the word determines the position of the outline.

Read the outlines and then write them several times.

The short sound of Ă (as in **bag**) is represented by a light dot. This dot is placed at the **beginning** of a stroke, either before or after it:

add adds adding added attack attacks attacking attacked act acts

acting acted cash cashed ago away fact Saturday adapt adapts

adapting adapted attach attaches attaching attached catch

afford affords afforded bad bank banks banking banked at

Read the outlines and then write them several times.

The sound of **AW** (as in **jaw**) is represented by a heavy dash written at the **beginning** of a stroke, either before or after it:

jaw jaws bought talk talks talking talked tall taller

cause causes causing caused caught thought small smaller

law laws lawyer saw saws walk walks walking walked

Read the outlines and then write them several times.

The short sound of Ŏ (as in **top**) is represented by a light dash. This dash is placed at the **beginning** of a stroke, either before or after it:

top tops topping topped dock docks loss losses not off

job jobs lot lots shop shops shopping shopped watch watches

watching watched wash washes washing washed got wrong was

or song songs long longs oppose because

Read the outlines and then write them several times.

Note that the four vowels **AH, Ă, AW, Ŏ** are all written in the **first** position. This means that the first downstroke or upstroke, in words in which these are the **first** vowel sounds, is written **above** the line.

Short Forms and Derivatives

ought owe/oh owes owing owed always also

although tomorrow

Phrases and Intersections
A single stroke may be written through another stroke to represent a frequently occurring word. When convenient stroke **CH** may be intersected for the word **charge,** and stroke **F** for the word **form:**

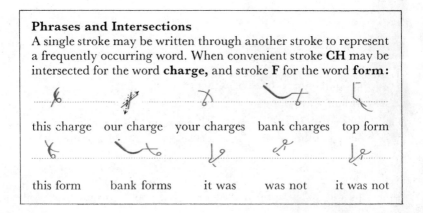

this charge our charge your charges bank charges top form

this form bank forms it was was not it was not

PRACTICE PLAN

1. Read through the exercise, referring to the key if necessary.
2. Practise writing any outline which caused any hesitancy in reading.
3. Write each sentence until you can write it easily and rapidly.
4. Write each sentence from dictation.
5. Read the sentences from your own shorthand notes.
6. Transcribe (by hand, until you can type) the exercise from the textbook as a homework assignment.

READING AND WRITING PRACTICE

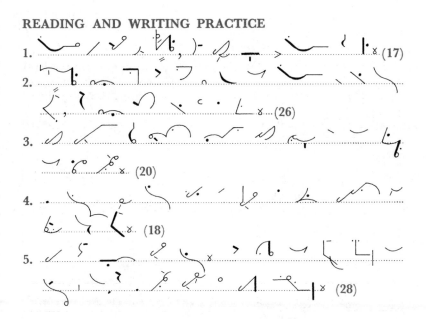

Key to Reading and Writing Practice

1. Banks are always shut on Saturdays, so we shall not go to the bank on that day. (**17**)
2. On Mondays you may get all the cash you have in the bank to pay for your shopping, although you may also pay with a cheque. (**26**)
3. We shall work on this smaller market and we shall let you know of any changes in the sales results. (**20**)
4. The firm is not far away and it was a shame we were not chosen for that job. (**18**)
5. We thought the game was fair. All the lads in the top form attacked in force but for all that the result was not as we had expected. (**28**)

READING AND WRITING PRACTICE (Contd.)

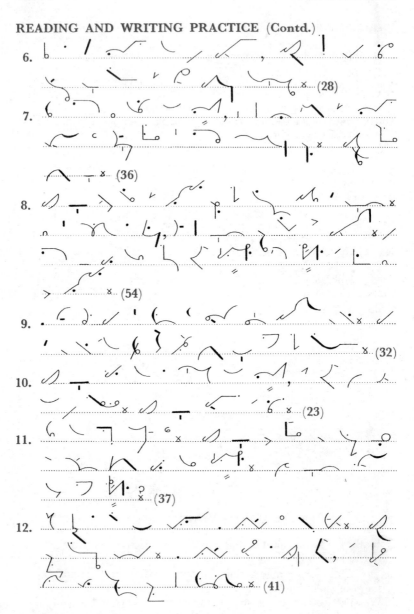

6. (28)

7. (36)

8. (54)

9. (32)

10. (23)

11. (37)

12. (41)

Key to Reading and Writing Practice (Contd.)

6. It is a large market for our work, and we shall be adding to our sales force to cut back on the losses we have had for months. **(28)**

7. This car is for sale in March, but it may not be on the market too long with so much tax on cars manufactured today. We think this form of tax will be cut. (**36**)

8. We shall go up the pass on the railway to stay at the farm and we think you ought to come. You owe yourself a change, so do come to this part of the world. Our car could wait for you at your shop on Wednesday or Saturday and take you to the railway. (**54**)

9. The law says we owe them that small sum and we will have to pay. We ought to pay off this charge although the result will be no cash at the bank. (**32**)

10. We shall go away for a month in March, and the shop will shut in our absence. We shall go walking and sailing. (**23**)

11. Thank you for getting in touch with us. We shall go to the docks to fetch the cases of rum which will be waiting for us on Wednesday. Will you come along for the cash on Saturday? (**37**)

12. I think it would be a bad thing to regard the report as being thorough. We shall have to check the facts tomorrow. The report was a rushed job, and it was left too late for them to check it themselves. (**41**)

SHORT FORM AND PHRASE DRILL

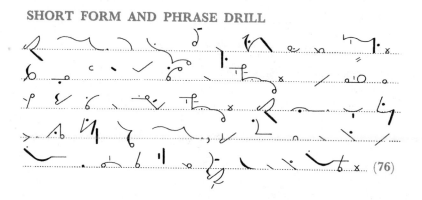

(76)

Key to Short Form and Phrase Drill

We shall be manufacturing your firm's saws today and they will be sent to you on Monday. This is the case with all of our sales to customers. Our success is such that we sell to export customers. We shall be making no change to the rates charged for this manufacturing, but we ask you to pay our bank the sum which is owed to us so that we shall not have to pay bank charges. (**76**)

UNIT 9
L hook to straight strokes:
PL, BL, TL, DL
CHL, JL, KL, GL
Circles to hooked strokes

A small hook at the beginning of a straight downstroke, **K** and **G,** written on the same side as the **circle S,** adds the sound of **L.** The double consonants **PL, BL, TL, DL, CHL, JL, KL, GL** are written:

play   plays   playing   played   place   places   placing   placed   blow

blows   able   apple   blank   close   closing   closed   claim   claims

claiming   glow   glows   glowing   class   clock   plate   plates

The hook **L** may also be used in the middle of an outline:

enable   enables   enabling   enabled   unable   table   tables   tabling

tabled   total   totals   totalling   totalled   enclose   encloses   enclosing model   meddle/medal   label   local   uncle   replace

replaces   replacing   replaced   sample   cudgel   muddle   muddled

A small dash written at the end of an outline adds the suffix **INGS**:

placing   placings   cutting   cuttings   shaving   shavings   saying   sayings

The sound of **S** is added to the **hook L** by writing the **circle S inside** the hook, at the beginning or in the middle of an outline:

saddle   settle   settled   satchel   explore   explores   exploring

explored   exclaim   exclaims   exclaiming   exclaimed

Read the outlines and then write them several times.

Always practise the short forms and phrases. Make sure you write them in their correct positions.

Short Forms and Derivatives

who   largely   able to

Phrases

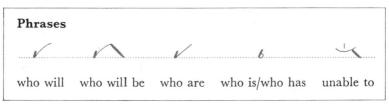

who will   who will be   who are   who is/who has   unable to

PRACTICE PLAN

1. Read through the exercise, referring to the key if necessary.
2. Practise writing any outline which caused any hesitancy in reading.
3. Write each sentence until you can write it easily and rapidly.
4. Write each sentence from dictation.
5. Read the sentences from your own shorthand notes.
6. Transcribe the reading and writing practice.

READING AND WRITING PRACTICE

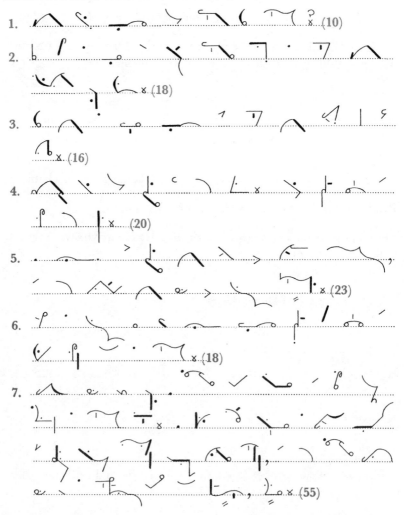

8.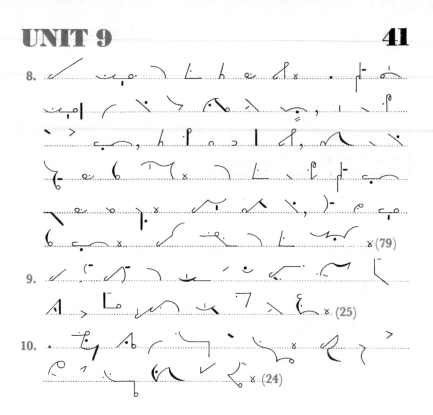

(79)

9.

(25)

10.

(24)

Key to Reading and Writing Practice

1. Who will be playing games for the club this month? (**10**)

2. It is largely a case of both clubs getting a coach who will be available to aid them. (**18**)

3. This will be a close game and the coach will be watching it with the lads. (**16**)

4. You will be able to pay for the tables with your cheque. Pay the total sum and settle your debt. (**20**)

5. The making of the tables will be up to the local manufacturer, and your report will be sent to the firm on Monday. (**23**)

6. Such a firm is able to make claims totalling large sums and they are settled in a month. (**18**)

7. We have sent to you today the samples of our bags and satchels for which you asked a month ago. The delay arose because a young girl on the despatch bench managed to get the labels muddled, and your samples were sent to a customer of ours in Dunmow, Essex. (**55**)

Key to Reading and Writing Practice (Contd.)

8. We are enclosing your cheque which you sent yesterday. The total sum enclosed will pay for the labels up to May, but to settle all of the claim, which you said you would do yesterday, you will have to pay for those sent this month. Your cheque to settle the total claim could be sent to us today. We know you are able to pay, so let us close this claim. We will expect your cheque in the mail. (**79**)

9. We thought we saw your uncle and aunt walking along the top road to the docks but we were unable to catch up with them. (**25**)

10. The exchange rates will affect all firms. We shall have to think of the losses and the effects they will have on our shops. (**24**)

SHORT FORM AND PHRASE DRILL

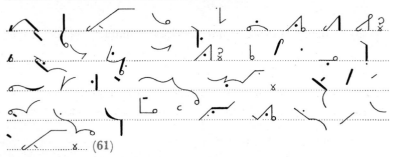

(61)

Key to Short Form and Phrase Drill

Who will be able to do this work for us today at the same rates we had yesterday? Who is to blame for the changes in the rate? It is largely a case of doing something which will aid all manufacturers in the market. Both large and small firms have had talks with regard to rates per hour for all work. (**61**)

UNIT 10
Diphthongs I and OI
Loops St and Ster
Md, Nd
Triphones

A diphthong is two vowel sounds pronounced as one. The diphthong **I** (as in **by**) is represented by the sign ⌄ written at the beginning, in the middle or at the end of an outline. The sign for **I** is written in the **first position**.

by/buy   buys   buying   time   times   timing   timed   mile

miles   mileage   life   my   might   light   lights   lighting   wide   nice

fire   fires   firing   fired   apply   applies   applying   applied

like   likes   liking   liked   desire   desires   desiring   desired

supply   supplies   supplying   supplied   guide   guides   guiding

guided   fight   fights   fighting   daylight   delight   delights

delighting   delighted

When a vowel other than **Ĕ** occurs between **S-S**, the vowel sign is placed in the circle. Circle **S** can be added to the **SES** circle.

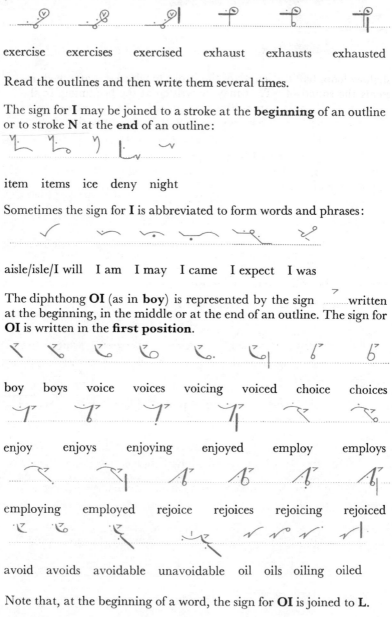

exercise   exercises   exercised   exhaust   exhausts   exhausted

Read the outlines and then write them several times.

The sign for **I** may be joined to a stroke at the **beginning** of an outline or to stroke **N** at the **end** of an outline:

item   items   ice   deny   night

Sometimes the sign for **I** is abbreviated to form words and phrases:

aisle/isle/I will   I am   I may   I came   I expect   I was

The diphthong **OI** (as in **boy**) is represented by the sign written at the beginning, in the middle or at the end of an outline. The sign for **OI** is written in the **first position**.

boy   boys   voice   voices   voicing   voiced   choice   choices

enjoy   enjoys   enjoying   enjoyed   employ   employs

employing   employed   rejoice   rejoices   rejoicing   rejoiced

avoid   avoids   avoidable   unavoidable   oil   oils   oiling   oiled

Note that, at the beginning of a word, the sign for **OI** is joined to **L**.

Read the outlines and then write them several times.

A small tick added to the diphthongs **I** or **OI** indicates any following vowel sound and the sign is called a triphone.

buyer   via   science   employee   voyage   dial   royal   enjoyable

A shallow loop, half the length of the stroke to which it is attached, represents the sound of **ST.** It may be written at the beginning, in the middle, or at the end of an outline **except** when the outline begins or ends with a vowel. The **ST** loop is written in the same direction as **circle S:**

stock   style   stop   most   next   just   lost   past   chest

store   stores   storing   stored   start   starts   starting   started   guest

Circle S can be added to the **ST loop:**

test   tests   testing   tested   suggest   suggests   suggesting

suggested   post   posts   posting   posted   last   lasts   lasting

lasted   rest   rests   resting   rested   burst   bursts   bursting

Note that downward **R** is used at the end of an outline when followed by the sound of **ST.**

The **ST** loop cannot be used if a vowel occurs between **S** and **T:** or if a vowel at the end of a word follows the sound of **ST.**

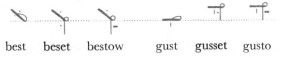

best   beset   bestow   gust   gusset   gusto

Read the outlines and then write them several times.

Stroke S is written at the **beginning** of an outline when it is immediately followed by a vowel and the sound of **S** or **Z**:

size   sizes   sauce   sauces   saucer   essays   says

Stroke S is retained in a word if the root outline is written with a stroke:

saw   sawdust   ice   icebox   sow/sew   sowed/sewed

Read the outlines and then write them several times.

The sound **STER** is represented by a large loop, two-thirds the length of a normal length stroke, in the middle or at the end of an outline. **Circle S** can be added to the **STER** loop:

master   mastering   mastered   faster   cluster   clusters   Leicester

Note the development of the loops from the **circle S**:

mass   masses   mast   masts   masters   pose   poses   post   posts

poster   posters

Strokes **M** and **N** are halved and thickened to add the following sound of **D**:

mad   made   mud   end   ends   ending   stand   stands   standing

Read the outlines and then write them several times.

Short Forms and Derivatives

immediate   immediately   should   without   influence   influencing

influenced   largest   several   almost   first

Always write the phrases several times before you begin the reading and writing practice.

Phrases

it should be   it should not be   you should   you should not

you should not be   at first   first time   for the first time   first class

as fast as   just as   always be

PRACTICE PLAN

1. Read through the exercise on the next page, referring to the key if necessary.
2. Practise writing any outline which caused any hesitancy in reading.
3. Write each sentence until you can write it easily and rapidly.
4. Write each sentence from dictation.
5. Read the sentences from your own shorthand notes.
6. Transcribe the reading and writing practice.

READING AND WRITING PRACTICE

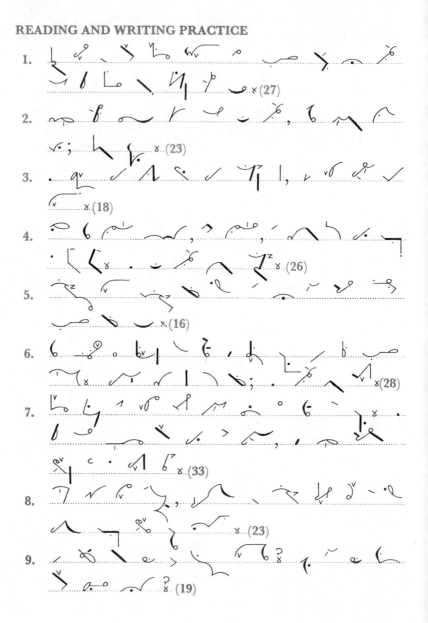

1. .... (27)

2. .... (23)

3. .... (18)

4. .... (26)

5. .... (16)

6. .... (28)

7. .... (33)

8. .... (23)

9. .... (19)

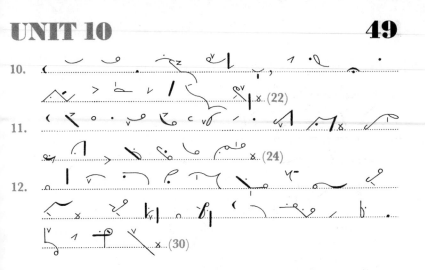

10.
11.
12.

Key to Reading and Writing Practice

1. It would be wise to buy the items that you like as the next budget may result in the largest tax being charged on such things. (**27**)

2. You must suggest something which will influence the end result, and this should not be left too late; it should be without delay. (**23**)

3. The first time we read the play we enjoyed it, but the style was not to our liking. (**18**)

4. Master this lesson immediately, and all the lessons, and you will be on your way to getting a top job. The end result will be enjoyable. (**26**)

5. Employers like to employ the best staff and may not always accept the next best thing. (**16**)

6. This exercise is designed for all those who desire to take our test next month. We know you will do your best; the result should be all right. (**28**)

7. Times change and the styles of yesterday are not the same as those of today. The largest influence comes by way of the young, who must always be supplied with a wide choice. (**33**)

8. Much oil lies offshore, but we will have to employ twice the size of staff we have to get supplies to this market. (**23**)

Key to Reading and Writing Practice (Contd.)

9. Should posters be sent to the firm like this? Should they not send them by the first-class mail? (**19**)

10. Without any influence the employer signed the note, and the staff made a report of the stock on the large form supplied. (**22**)

11. That boy has a nice voice with style and a wide range. We must send the lad to the best place for his lessons. (**24**)

12. You had my car last month because I thought something was wrong. I was delighted you suggested that your experts should test the tyres and the exhaust pipe. (**30**)

SHORT FORM AND PHRASE DRILL

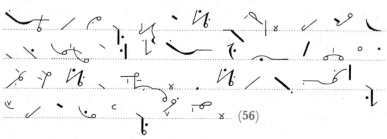

Key to Short Form and Phrase Drill

Bank charges are less today but we think that all charges could be stopped. We always have to pay for some forms of aid at the bank and they make large sums as a result of such charges to customers. The charges are being cancelled to aid the fight we all face with today's rising costs. (**56**)

R hook to straight strokes:
PR, BR, TR, DR
CHR, JR, KR, GR
Circles and loops to hooks

A small hook written on the left-hand side at the beginning of a straight downstroke, and underneath horizontals adds the sound of **R**:

present   presents   presenting   presented   price   prices   pricing

priced   prepare   prepares   preparing   prepared   branch   branches

branching   branched   draw   draws   drawing   grow   grows   growing

try   tries   trying   tried   trust   trusts   trusting   address

addresses   addressing   addressed   across   brought

The **hook R** is also used in the middle of an outline:

surprise   surprises   surprised   regret   regrets   regretted

Read the outlines and then write them several times.

The **R** hook is also used for the syllables **per, ber, ter, der, cher, jer, ker, ger:**

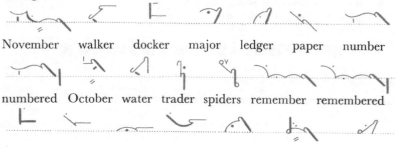

November   walker   docker   major   ledger   paper   number

numbered   October   water   trader   spiders   remember   remembered

dagger   packer   maker   banker   labour   December   searcher

When an unstressed vowel occurs between the consonant stroke and the sound of **R,** the **hook R** is used and the vowel is omitted:

correct   corrects   correcting   corrected

In the following outlines the **hook R** is used and the **strongly** sounded vowel is omitted:

course/coarse   courses   court   courts   record   recording   recorded

To add the sound of **S** at the **beginning** of straight strokes hooked for **R,** close the hook: **SPR**   **STR**   **SCR** :

spray   sprays   stress   stresses   straight   scrape   scraped

When **SCR** or **SGR** follows **T, D, P** or **B** the hook and circle are written:

describe   prescribe   subscribe   Tasker

Read the outlines and then write them several times.

When a vowel occurs between **circle S** or **ST loop** and a straight stroke hooked for **R**, the **circle S** or **ST loop** is written on the same side as the **R** hook:

supper   cider   sober   soccer   separate   stutter   stoker

When the sounds of **SPR, STR** occur in the **middle** of a word, **circle S** is written **inside** the hook:

express   extra   destroy

Read the outlines and then write them several times.

Short Forms and Derivatives

dear   larger   accord/according/according to   particular

particulars   trade/toward   towards

Phrases
Note that in the phrase **for some time,** the **circle S** between two curved strokes is written **inside** the **first** curve, and that the first **M** is halved to represent the **T** in **time.**

Dear Sir   of course   in the course of   at present   at some time

for some time   yours faithfully   yours sincerely   I regret

When convenient intersect stroke **K** for **company** and strokes **K** and **L** joined for **company limited:**

this company   your company   Paper Company Limited

PRACTICE PLAN

1. Read through the exercise, referring to the key if necessary.
2. Practise writing any outline which caused any hesitancy in reading.
3. Write each sentence until you can write it easily and rapidly.
4. Write each sentence from dictation.
5. Read the sentences from your own shorthand notes.
6. Transcribe the reading and writing practice.

READING AND WRITING PRACTICE

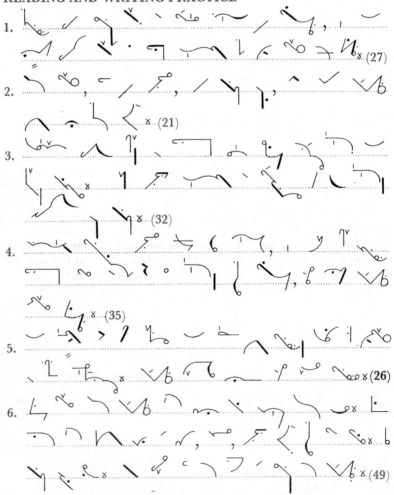

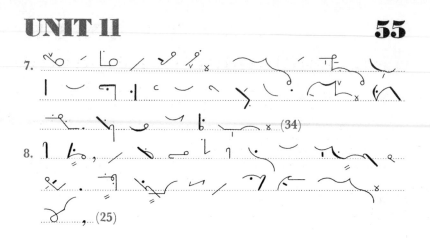

7.

8.

Key to Reading and Writing Practice

1. At present we spread the buying of products among our branches, but in March we will buy a great number at the low prices your company charges. (**27**)
2. All your prices, according to our records, are better today, and all of our purchases will be made at your shop. (**21**)
3. For some time we have tried to correct some strange errors occurring in typed papers. I do regret the number of problems which have occurred, and we will have to do better. (**32**)
4. I am unable to prepare the records for the company this month, but I shall try to present correct particulars of all that has occurred at this branch, such as major purchases and price changes. (**35**)
5. In October all the larger items in stock will be presented for sale at low prices to attract customers. Purchases like this make such nice presents. (**26**)
6. Check the price of your purchases or you may pay too much for your things. Take care or it will be too late and you will, of course, regret shopping at this particular place. It is better to play safe. Be wise with your cash and spread your purchasing. (**49**)
7. Prices and taxes are always rising. Manufacturers and customers have not had any great aid with any particular budget for a long time. They will be expecting better things in the days to come. (**34**)
8. Dear James,
   Our best course at the trade fair in November is to support the Exeter Paper Company Limited—our major local manufacturer. Yours sincerely, (**25**)

READING AND WRITING PRACTICE (Contd.)

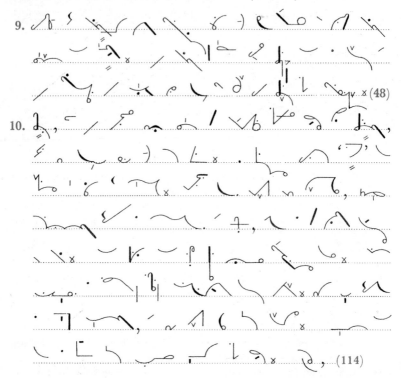

9. ... (48)

10. ... (114)

Key to Reading and Writing Practice (Contd.)

9. We trust that the Paper Company Limited will be prepared to sell us several boxes of ledger paper some time in October. Our paper stock was destroyed in a fire and our branches are unable to let us have the particular sizes we desire at the present time. (**48**)

10. Dear Sir,
   According to our records you made some large purchases at our company's stores last December, and yet you have not sent us your cheque. The terms were 'Cash' for items on sale that month. I regret having to write to you like this, but you must remember that we are a manufacturing and trading company, and have a large labour force to pay. Any delay in settling debts makes problems for us. I am enclosing a stamped addressed envelope for your reply. You will note that we have a code number, and you should write this on your files. Come in for a talk on your next call at the store.
   Yours faithfully, (**114**)

SHORT FORM AND PHRASE DRILL

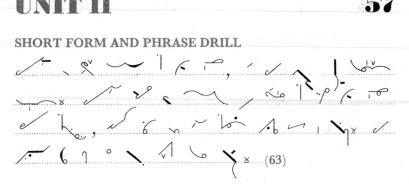

(63)

Key to Short Form and Phrase Drill

We are glad to supply anything at low cost, and we should be able to do so for some time to come. We are not always able to manufacture our products at such low costs as we are at present, and we will sell to you not at the same rates—but better. We regard this trade as being right for us both. (**63**)

ADDITIONAL READING AND WRITING PRACTICE

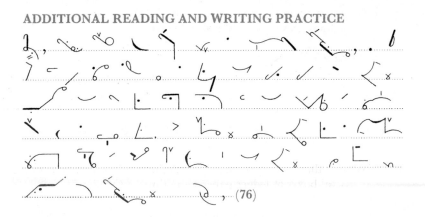

(76)

Key to Additional Reading and Writing Practice

Dear Sir,

Present prices have brought to light a number of problems, the largest of which according to our sales staff is a change in the way we all shop. Girls in particular take great care with any purchases and seldom buy without a close checking of the items. Some shoppers take a long time to select clothes and always try them on in the shop. Let us talk to you regarding your problems.

Yours faithfully, (**76**)

UNIT 12
Third-place vowels
Ē, Ĭ, ŌŌ, ŎŎ
Position writing
Stroke Z
Diphones

In the following examples the first downstroke or upstroke is written **through** the line. This is called the **third position.**

The long sound of Ē (as in **please**) is represented by a heavy dot written at the **end** of a stroke:

piece   pieces   please   pleases   pleasing   pleased   eat   eats   eating   she

see   sees   seeing   key   agree   tree   each   lease   teas   feet

Read the outlines and then write them several times.

When a third-place vowel comes between two strokes it is written in the third position in front of the second stroke:

teach   teaches   teaching   reach   reaches   reaching   reached   fear

deep   deepest   deeper   deal   deals   dealing   leave   leaves   leaving meal   team   people   clear   keep   appeal   succeed   believe

Notice again that in words like **meal** and **keep,** it is the first upstroke or downstroke that is written **through** the line.

Read the outlines and then write them several times.

The sound of the short vowel Ĭ (as in **if**) is represented by a light dot written at the **end** of a stroke:

if   ill   sit   bill   bring   did   city   citizen   list   lists   listed   simple

simplest   simpler   simply   figure   limit   big   bigger   biggest   wish

apology   apologies   apologize   statistics   artistic   visit   visiting

build   buildings   bid   bids   instead   indeed   fit   little   elastic   possible

impossible   built   liberal   factory   lady   family   monthly   many

copy   lucky   daily   money   width   thick   spirit   insert   inserting

inserted   system   sister   necessary

Read the outlines and then write them several times.

The long sound of O̅O̅ (as in **blue**) is represented by a heavy dash written at the **end** of a stroke:

blue   truth   July   use   useless   lose/loose   move   group   cool   shoe   food

The short sound of **ŎŌ** (as in **book**) is represented by a light dash written at the **end** of a stroke:

book wool foot look full pull cook push stood took

Read the outlines and then write them several times.

POSITION WRITING

When the third-place vowel sound **ĒĒ, Ĭ, ŌŌ** or **ŎŌ** is the first in a word, the first downstroke or upstroke is written through the line. When there is no downstroke or upstroke the outline is written on the line:

increase sing mood good mist miss missed Mrs

Z is a thick curved downstroke   . When **Z** is the first or only consonant sound in a word use **stroke Z**:

ooze zoo zero ease eases easing eased

When a vowel sound follows **S** or **Z** at the end of a word, stroke **S** or **Z** is used:

cosy lazy daisy posy rosy policy

Circle S for the sound of **S** or **Z** may be written in the middle of an outline:

business businesses loser razor

Read the outlines and then write them several times.

UNIT 12 61

DOUBLE-VOWEL SIGNS (DIPHONES)

When two vowel sounds follow each other, they are shown by the sign
⌄ , making what is called a diphone. Write this sign in the position of
the first vowel sound in the diphone:

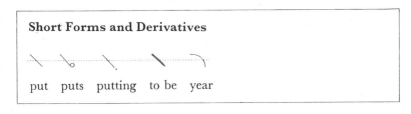

idea   ideal   ideally   piano   radio   area   create   co-operate   earlier

earliest   previous   obvious   premium   medium   really   realize

agreeable   glorious   serious   lower   lowest   jewel

Read the outlines and then write them several times.

Short Forms and Derivatives

put   puts   putting   to be   year

Phrases

When convenient **stroke B** and **circle S** ⟍ᵒ is intersected for
business.

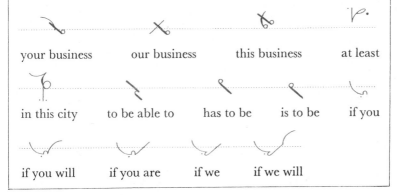

your business   our business   this business   at least

in this city   to be able to   has to be   is to be   if you

if you will   if you are   if we   if we will

62

PRACTICE PLAN

1. Read through the exercise, referring to the key if necessary.
2. Practise writing any outline which caused any hesitancy in reading.
3. Write each sentence until you can write it easily and rapidly.
4. Write each sentence from dictation.
5. Read the sentences from your own shorthand notes.
6. Transcribe the reading and writing practice.

READING AND WRITING PRACTICE

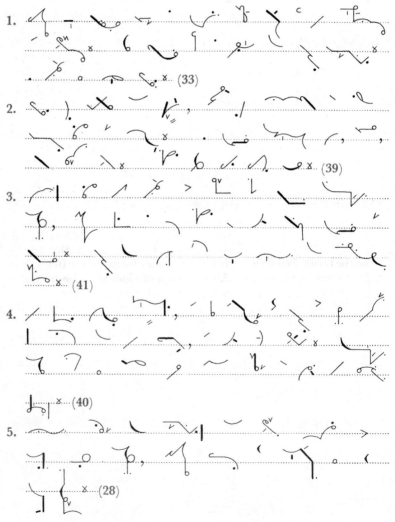

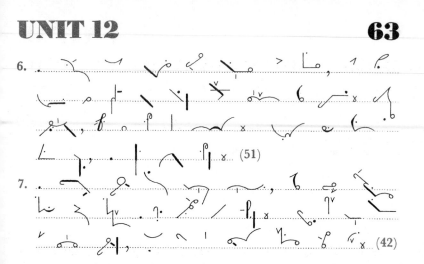

6. ... (51)

7. ... (42)

Key to Reading and Writing Practice

1. We think it is good business to create a feeling of trust both with our customers and suppliers. This brings with it a reason for people to co-operate. The result is most pleasing. (**33**)

2. Please see to our business in July, and use each member of staff to keep sales on the move. The figures for the month will, of course, be slightly up. At least this is the way we see things. (**39**)

3. Limited sales are the result of the strike at the big factory in this city, and I think it will take a year at least to show better figures on the books. People have little or no money for expensive items. (**41**)

4. Our team leaves on Monday, and it is obvious that the people of the city really do care for our group, and show us support. Victory in this match is almost ours and any ideas of losing are simply dismissed. (**40**)

5. Many areas have co-operated in supplying meals to the needy cases in this city, and we think it is clear that nobody is without food at this time. (**28**)

6. The error in the bills was because of the tax, and the last figure is the total to be paid by the company some time this week. We think it is reasonable, and suggest you settle it immediately. If you will send them a cheque today, the debt will be settled. (**51**)

7. The group uses far too much money, and this creates problems at the end of the year at the time the trading results are studied. Please try to cut back on the sums used, in particular on small items such as lighting. (**42**)

READING AND WRITING PRACTICE (Contd.)

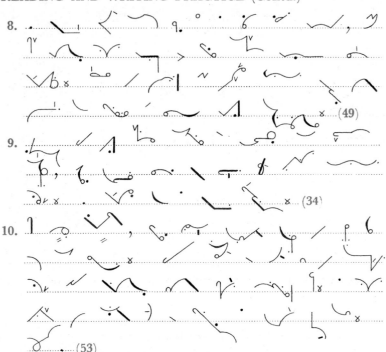

8.

9.

10.

Key to Reading and Writing Practice (Contd.)

8. The book shop in your street has a sale starting tomorrow, and I shall try to leave early to get to the place in time to make some purchases. Stocks are limited and I realize that many people will be looking for presents and something to read for themselves. (**49**)

9. Each month we read items in the press of increases in crime in this city, and these figures seem to be growing just as rapidly in many areas. The police have a big problem. (**34**)

10. Dear Mrs Barber,
   Please let us know if you are able to visit our city this year in the spring. We are anxious to show you our factory area and we believe you will be truly impressed with it. An early reply will enable us to prepare a full tour for you.
   Yours sincerely, (**53**)

SHORT FORM AND PHRASE DRILL

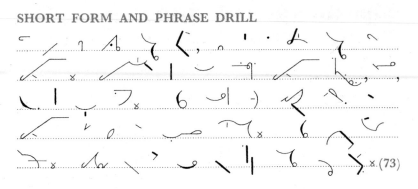

Key to Short Form and Phrase Drill

According to our trade rates for this job, you owe a large sum for this particular work. We are unable to do any extra work at present, of course, having had no cash. This has influenced us and we shall be stopping all work on the first of next month. This will be the fault of your company. We think you should put all the things to be added in this year's budget. **(73)**

ADDITIONAL READING AND WRITING PRACTICE

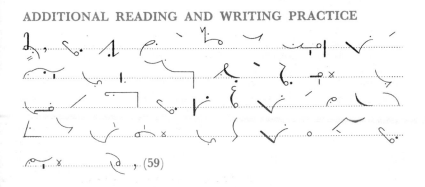

Key to Additional Reading and Writing Practice

Dear Sir,
Please read the list of items in the enclosed bill and let me know if you did in fact receive all of these goods. If the figures are correct please deal with this bill and let us have your cheque for the full sum. If you think the bill is wrong please let us know.
Yours faithfully, **(59)**

UNIT 13
Diphthongs OW and U
Triphones
ZH and H

The diphthong **OW** (as in **out**) is represented by the sign ⌄ written in the third position at the beginning, in the middle or at the end of an outline. When **OW** is the **first** vowel sound in a word, the outline is written in the **third** position:

out south loud crowd crowds allow allows announce announces

A small tick added to the diphthong **OW** indicates any following vowel sound and the sign is called a triphone:

power powers powerless tower towers shower showers

The diphthong **OW** may sometimes be joined to a stroke, and such strokes may be halved for **T** or **D**:

doubt spout about proud bout tout

When the sound of **S** is added to these words, the diphthong **OW** is not joined and the halving rule for one-syllable words is followed. A **light** stroke may only be halved for T, and a **heavy** stroke may only be halved for **D**:

doubts bouts spouts touts

Read the outlines and then write them several times.

UNIT 13

The diphthong **U** (as in **duty**) is represented by the sign ⌒ written in the third position at the beginning, in the middle or at the end of an outline. When **U** is the **first** vowel sound, the outline is written in the third position. The **U** sign may be joined to a stroke, and a single stroke outline may be halved for **T** or **D**. When the sound of **S** is added to these words the diphthong **U** is not joined, and the halving rule for one-syllable words is followed:

duty   beauty   refuse   refuses   secure   secures   presume   presumes

few   view   views   knew/new   news   newspaper   Tuesday   issue

issues   value   values   assume   assumes   feud   feuds   mute   mutes

A small tick added to the diphthong **U** indicates any following vowel sound and the sign is called a triphone:

valuable   fewer   duet   reviewer   mutual

Read the outlines and then write them several times.

The sound **ZH** (as in **usual**) is a thick curved downstroke :

usual   usually   azure   mirage   garage

Read the outlines and then write them several times.

The sound of **H** is represented by the sign written **upwards**:

UNIT 13

hotel head whose hike hot hotter hottest heat hurry

house   houses   habit   hero   perhaps

Read the outlines and then write them several times.

> Note the difference between the writing of **circle S** before upward **R,** and the writing of **H** as in:
>
> sorry   high

When it is not possible to write an upward **H** in the middle of an outline the **H** is omitted:

household   leasehold   mishap

The sound of **H** occurring before **M, L** and downward **R** at the **beginning** of a word is represented by a light tick written **downwards** from right to left :

home homes him himself her herself holiday holidays health

healthy hold held hair hire hired hill hurt heart

whole/hole   wholesome   hear/here   help   helper   helplessness

Read the outlines and then write them several times.

Remember to practise the short forms and phrases.
Make sure you write them in their correct positions.

Short Forms and Derivatives

how   subject   subjects   subjected   subjecting

Phrases

New York   he is   he will   he will be   he was

A heavy tick, written downwards, may be used for the word **he** in the middle or at the end of a phrase:

if he will   if he will be   if he   if he is   I think he will

The stroke **P** may be used to represent the word **hope** in phrases:

we hope   I hope   I hope that   I hope that the

PRACTICE PLAN

1. Read through the exercise, referring to the key if necessary.
2. Practise writing any outline which caused any hesitancy in reading.
3. Write the sentences from dictation until you can write them easily and rapidly.
4. Read your own shorthand notes.
5. Transcribe the reading and writing practice from your own shorthand notes.

READING AND WRITING PRACTICE

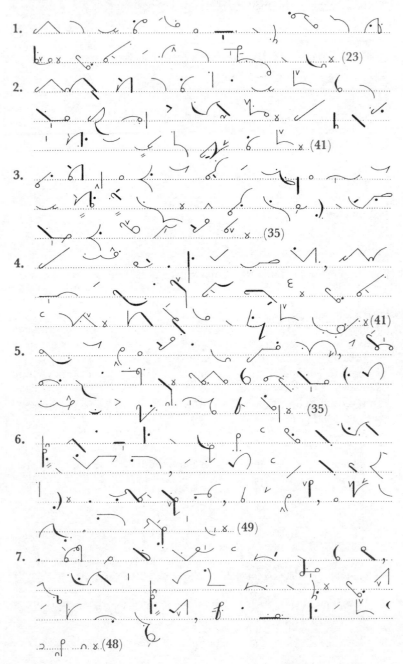

1.

2.

3.

4.

5.

6.

7.

8.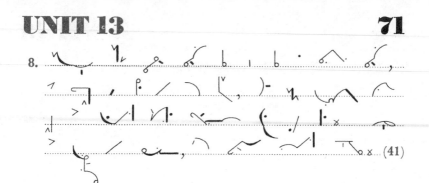

Key to Reading and Writing Practice

1. We hope your new sales office is going to issue samples of your latest designs. Please hurry and allow your customers to view. (**23**)
2. We hope you will be able to hold your sale at a new time this year because we shall have missed all the valuable items. We are due to be away on holiday in New York at your usual sale time. (**41**)
3. He sold out his share in the hotel and invested his money in the new Holidays Abroad firm. How he will fare is not easy to forecast because the share prices are not always high. (**35**)
4. We are announcing soon the date of our next party, and we hope you will come and bring a bright young group with you. Please hurry with your reply. It will be possible for us to change the time if necessary.´ (**41**)
5. Spring in the south is always a few weeks earlier, and the blossoms seem to have an extra beauty. Perhaps this is simply because they also announce the end of the dreary months just passed. (**35**)
6. Tuesday should be a good day to visit the city with space being available to park the car, and also with our being able to shop at ease. The neighbourhood beside the castle, which is on the south side, is ideal for leaving the car and proceeding on foot. (**49**)
7. The solicitor is the best person with whom to discuss this subject, and if he is available on Tuesday I will ask him to see you. Please write and tell me if this is not all right, and suggest an exact day and time that would suit you. (**48**)
8. I have no idea whose hotel it is but it is a happy hotel, and the crowd who stay are your type, so I doubt if you will be left out of the varied holiday programme they have each day. Most of the visitors are single, or young married couples. (**41**)

READING AND WRITING PRACTICE (Contd.)

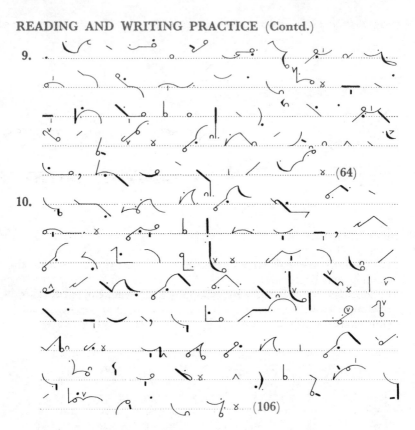

9. ... (64)

10. ... (106)

Key to Reading and Writing Practice (Contd.)

9. The value of antiques is always increasing and for this reason you should invest some of your spare money in a few items. Go to a good dealer because it is his duty to see that you pay a reasonable price and choose wisely. He will help you and show you how to avoid fakes, which may be things of beauty but are valueless. (64)

10. If he is to keep himself healthy he will have to break the habit of smoking. He knows it is doing him no good, and we hope he will hear and take your strict advice. We know your views are sound and we believe he will be happy to be advised by you. It might be a good thing too, if he takes regular exercise and tries to reduce weight. No doubt he thinks he is healthy but he will be sorry if he assumes that he knows best. How easy it is to choose wholesome food and at the same time lose a few inches. (106)

SHORT FORM AND PHRASE DRILL

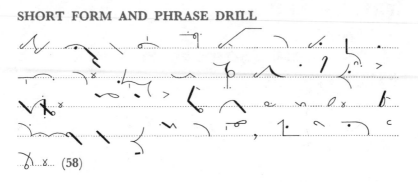

Key to Short Form and Phrase Drill

We think we may be able to put some extra work your way during the coming year. Each month now in this city we have a larger share of the building business. Almost all of the jobs will be sent to you first. Just remember to be sure about your costs, and take particular care with your charges. (58)

ADDITIONAL READING AND WRITING PRACTICE

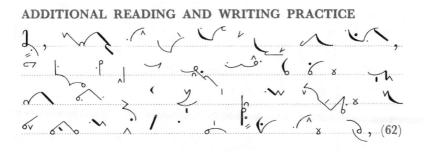

Key to Additional Reading and Writing Practice

Dear Sir,
I hope you will be able to allow full value on the vehicle we have available, according to the terms set out in the newspaper announcing this sale. No doubt you will be happy to hear that I shall know on Tuesday about the hire purchase. I have high hopes about how large a sum they will allow.
Yours faithfully, (62)

UNIT 14
Downward L
N hook
Circles and loops to N hook
Suffix -ment

L is written downward after **N, N halved** and **NG**:

only   unless   nil   annual   annually   unload   until   eventually

canal   recently   analyze   analysis   wrongly

Read the outlines and then write them several times.

The sound **INGLY** at the end of a word is represented by **NG** and **downward L**:

increasingly   exceedingly   unwillingly

N HOOK

A **small** hook written inside the **end** of a curved stroke adds the sound of **N**:

align   alone   then   known   men   man   often   than   opinion

mean   thin   within   vein   mine   lane   genuine   noon   fine

Read the outlines and then write them several times.

The **circle S** is written **inside** the **hook N** at the end of **curved** strokes for the sound of **NZ**:

earns   lines   machines   telephones   examines   woman's   humans

A **small** hook at the **end** of a straight stroke, written on the opposite side to the **circle S** adds **N**:

again   can   run   plain/plane   one/won   between   happen   maintain

town   eastern   western   garden   certain

Hook N is **not** used when a vowel follows **N** at the end of a word:

fun **but** funny   men **but** many   shine **but** shiny   bone **but** bony

A finally hooked thin or thick stroke is halved to add the sound of **T** or **D**. The **circle S** is written inside the **hook N** at the end of half-length curved strokes for the final sound of **S** or **Z**:

mind   mints   demand   payments   settlement   lands   event

Hook N may also be used in the **middle** of an outline:

arrange   arranges   plenty   apparently   finance   economy

maintenance   unfortunately   certainty   opportunity

Upward R is halved at the **beginning** of an outline if it is finally hooked:

rent   round

Read the outlines and then write them several times.

The sound of **NS** or **NZ** is shown by closing the hook on straight strokes **only**:

begin begins engine engines turn turns burn burns return returns

A finally hooked thin or thick stroke may be halved to add **T** or **D**:

spend spends important intelligent intelligence extend extends

second seconds disappoint disappoints account accounts evident

The sound of **S, SES, ST** or **STER** is added to a straight stroke hooked for **N** by writing the circle or loop on the same side as the **hook N**:

dance dances spin spins spinster spinsters again against

After curved strokes the sound of **NZ** is shown by **hook N** and **circle S**:

fens means nouns assigns balloons Romans

After curved strokes the sounds of **NS, NSES, NSTER** are shown by **stroke N** and the circle or loop:

fence fences monster announce essence balance romance

To make an easier joining ⌣ instead of ⌢ is sometimes used for **-MENT**:

appointment announcement department

-LY is sometimes written by disjoining the stroke **L**:

urgently suddenly certainly

Read the outlines and then write them several times.

Short Forms and Derivatives

cannot	responsible/ responsibility	gentleman	gentlemen

particularly	accordingly

Phrases

In phrases the word **not** is formed by halving the preceding stroke and adding the **N hook**. When the phrase **are not** cannot be joined to a preceding stroke, the full outline must be used :

you are   you are not   I can   I cannot   we can   we cannot   had not

do not   did not   you will not   I am   I am not   it will not

it will not be   I will not be

I went   at once   business man

When convenient intersect **downward R** for **arrange, arranged, arrangement** and stroke **D** for **department:**

this arrangement   we will arrange   he has arranged

I have arranged   your department   sales department

PRACTICE PLAN

1. Read through the exercise, referring to the key if necessary.
2. Practise writing any outline which caused any hesitancy in reading.
3. Write each sentence from dictation.
4. Read the sentences from your own shorthand notes.
5. Transcribe from your own shorthand notes.

READING AND WRITING PRACTICE

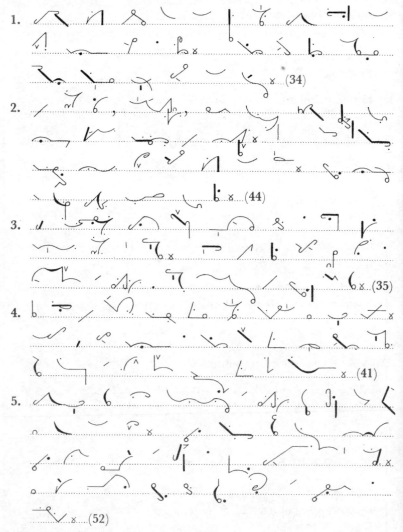

1.   (34)

2.   (44)

3.   (35)

4.   (41)

5.   (52)

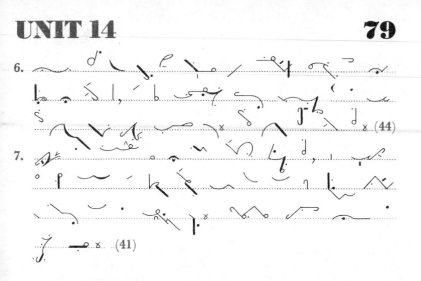

6. .... (44)

7. .... (41)

Key to Reading and Writing Practice

1. We cannot be held responsible for any debts unless we have agreed in writing to make such a settlement. Payment upon demand in this case cannot be made because no arrangement was in force. (34)
2. Our annual sale, unfortunately, is now finished but you will not be disappointed if you make the journey to examine our merchandise. I cannot begin to explain the many lines always held in stock. Please make arrangements to visit within the next few days. (44)
3. Gentlemen increasingly wear brighter colours and spend a great deal of money annually on clothes. Gone are the days of one suit lasting a long time and certainly the clothing manufacturers are pleased about this. (35)
4. It is against our policy to accept cheques unless the person is known to our company. Anyone who wants to make a payment by cheque must submit notice of this fact and allow time to clear the cheque at the bank. (41)
5. We have known this man for many years and certainly think he is trained for the job you have in mind. He began with this firm immediately he left school and joined a team working on engines. His whole career has been spent on these machines and he is now an expert. (52)
6. Many chances have been lost because our export department simply cannot meet the demands made upon it, and it is increasingly clear to management that a new plant will have to be built within the next year. Plans will be drawn up at once. (44)
7. Usually an announcement is made about policy changes at once, but no-one has said anything and it will not be possible now for any trade department report to appear in a newspaper today. Perhaps we can make an intelligent guess. (41)

SHORT FORM AND PHRASE DRILL

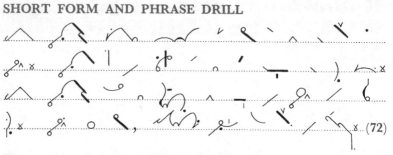

Key to Short Form and Phrase Drill

We hope he will be able to help you immediately on the subject of how to buy a house. He will be at our sales department and you ought to go to see him. We hope he will be able to influence you so that you will see how good our houses are on this estate. Housing is his subject, and we think you will see the reason for buying our property. (**72**)

ADDITIONAL READING AND WRITING PRACTICE

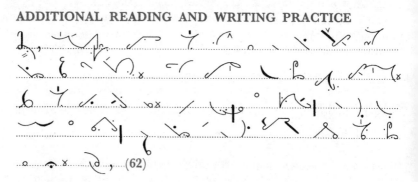

Key to Additional Reading and Writing Practice

Dear Sir,
Unfortunately we can only allow you to pay by one annual payment with this particular policy. Accordingly we must have settlement within one month. This is the only way open to us. Our finance department has telephoned to see if anything has happened to this payment and to say that we cannot be responsible unless settlement is made. Yours faithfully, (**62**)

UNIT 15
R hook to curved strokes
FR, VR, Thr, THR, SHR, ZHR
MR, NR

A **small** hook written **inside** and at the **beginning** of a curved stroke adds the sound of **R**:

free	frees/freeze	fruit	Friday	through/threw	throat

The hook **R** is also used for the syllables **fer, ver, ther, THer, sher, zher, mer** and **ner** at the beginning, in the middle and at the end of an outline. When an unstressed vowel occurs between the consonant stroke and the sound of R, the **hook R** is used and the vowel is omitted:

forget	forgotten	offer	offered	pressure	measure	measuring

measured	measurement	treasure	differ	different	difference

over	other	otherwise	favour	favourable	pleasure	leisure

murmur	manner/manor	mineral	funeral	average

Circle S is written **inside hook R** attached to curved strokes at the beginning of an outline:

savour	savoury	sever	summer	simmer	suffer	sooner

Read the outlines and then write them several times.

Fer, ver, ther, THer are always reversed **after** horizontal strokes and upstrokes. The reverse forms are written ⟍ ⟍)) :

cover gather weather however wafer recover silver government

Short Forms

together altogether satisfactory very there/their more before

from   commercial/commercially

Phrases

very little   very much   how much   it is certain   there is

there are   there will be   there is no   there are no

The words **than, been** and **own** are represented in a phrase by adding the **hook N**:

more than better than have been had been our own your own

PRACTICE PLAN

1. Read through the exercise, referring to the key if necessary.
2. Practise writing any outline which caused any hesitancy in reading.
3. Write each sentence from dictation.
4. Read the sentences from your own shorthand notes.
5. Transcribe the exercise from your own shorthand notes.

READING AND WRITING PRACTICE

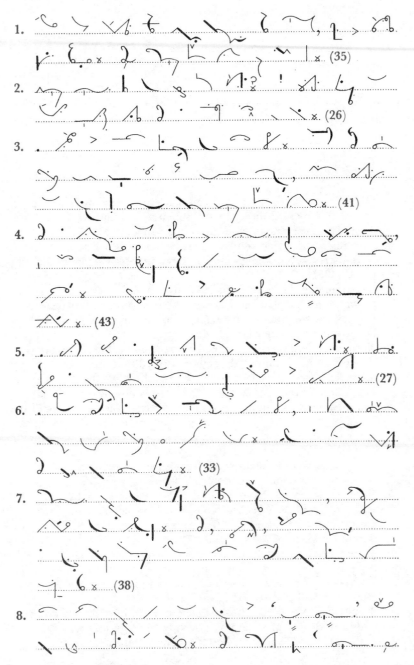

1. _____ (35)

2. _____ (26)

3. _____ (41)

4. _____ (43)

5. _____ (27)

6. _____ (33)

7. _____ (38)

8. _____

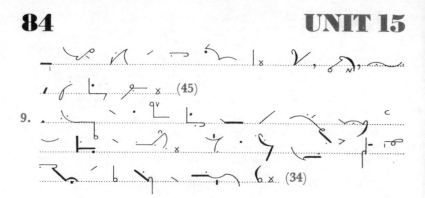

Key to Reading and Writing Practice

1. Offers for the purchase of this company should be made before the end of this month, direct to the solicitors dealing with this case. There is not very much time left to think about it. (**35**)

2. How much money do you have to spend on your holiday? Owing to certain changes in foreign currency rates there is an extra amount to pay. (**26**)

3. The results of the commercial take-over have been more than satisfactory. I gather that there is some pressure now to go ahead with the next move, and I am certainly in favour of doing something before too much time elapses. (**41**)

4. There is a reference in the statement to the many differences between the groups, but I am not altogether satisfied that these are anything more than commercial rumours. Please check all the recent statements in the Press together with the latest company report. (**43**)

5. The weather was a disappointment right from the beginning of the holiday. It seems that it was a poor summer in many different parts of the world. (**27**)

6. The strong measures taken by the government are satisfactory, but it will be some time before the full pressure is really felt. Over a long period there is bound to be some change. (**33**)

7. Very many people have enjoyed holidays arranged by this firm, and very satisfactory reports have been received. There is, however, always room for an even better package offer and some measures should be taken to look into this. (**38**)

8. More and more people are in favour of the 'No Smoking' signs to be found on trains and buses. There is very little doubt that smoking is not good for one's health and can harm it. There are, however, many who still take the risk. (**45**)

9. The effects of a strike taken together are impossible to measure with any degree of accuracy. Only an average figure of the total costs can be made and it is better to ignore this. (**34**)

SHORT FORM AND PHRASE DRILL

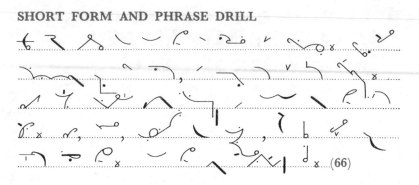

(66)

Key to Short Form and Phrase Drill

This company cannot be responsible for any loss of articles on the premises. Please always remember to take particular care, and keep your eye on your property. You are the only person who will be affected should anything be lost or stolen. You will not, of course, necessarily have insurance, although it is wise to have cover against losses. Any loss should be reported at once. (66)

ADDITIONAL READING AND WRITING PRACTICE

(58)

Key to Additional Reading and Writing Practice

Dear Sir,
Too much pressure from the sales department can result in either reduced sales or the total loss of a sale. More satisfactory offers should be made over the summer period so that we can discover how much this market is worth. The difference between sales here and in other areas is more than expected.
Yours faithfully, (58)

UNIT 16
L hook to curved strokes: FL, VL, ThL, ML, NL, SHL
The omission of vowels

A **large** hook at the beginning of a curved stroke adds the sound of **L** (as in **flow** or **camel**). The double consonants **FL, VL, ThL, ML, NL** and **SHL** are written:

flow	camel	penal	flannel	facial	flower	approval	travel

travelling	traveller	Ethel	partial	initial	final	finals

finalize	finally	helpful	helpfully	hopeful	hopefully

powerful	powerfully	official	officially	beautiful	beautifully

special	specially	especial	especially

When an unstressed vowel occurs between the consonant stroke and the sound of **L**, the **hook L** is used and the vowel is omitted:

fulfil	philosophy

Read the outlines and then write them several times.

Reversed forms of **FL** and **VL** are **always** used after horizontal strokes and upstrokes. The reverse forms are written ⟋⟍ :

reflect   reflects   reflecting   muffle   muffles   marvel   marvels

marvellous   level   novel   naval   rival   rivals

Read the outlines and then write them several times.

Short Forms and Derivatives

enlarge   enlarged   enlarges   enlarging   enlarger   enlargement

influential

Phrases and Intersections

as early as possible   as soon as   as soon as it is

as soon as possible   as soon as we can   as soon as we know

it is possible it is not possible United States United States of America

Note that when convenient stroke **Th** for **month** may be intersected or joined.

some months   next month   several months   this month

88 UNIT 16

PRACTICE PLAN

1. Read through the exercise, referring to the key if necessary.
2. Practise writing any outline which caused any hesitancy in reading.
3. Write each sentence from dictation until you can write it easily and rapidly.
4. Read the sentences from your own shorthand notes.
5. Transcribe the sentences from your own shorthand notes.

READING AND WRITING PRACTICE

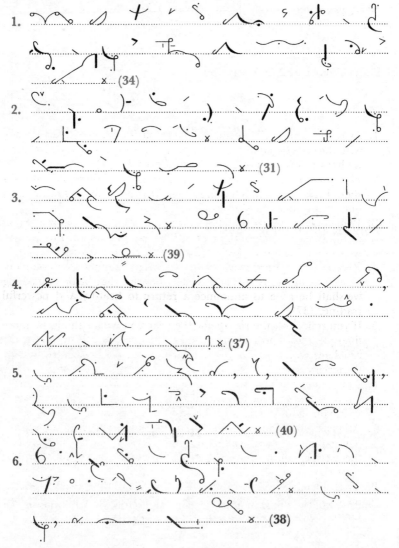

7.

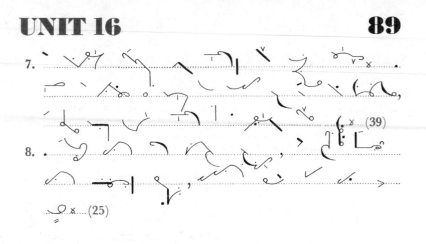

8.

Key to Reading and Writing Practice

1. As early as possible we shall enlarge on the plans we have made with the sales department to travel overseas to visit all the customers we have in many different areas of the world. (**34**)

2. Flying today is so fast and easy to arrange that these official visits should take place much more often. It is possible we shall extend our programme of visits next year. (**31**)

3. I am hopeful that we shall have the new and enlarged plant working at full capacity before the end of the year. As soon as this is done we can double our exports to the United States of America. (**39**)

4. Recent developments have been more than helpful to our company as well as to our rivals, and we feel hopeful that before very long we shall be able to announce a return to healthy and powerful trading. (**37**)

5. If you reflect on the results for the year you will, I think, be more than pleased, especially if you take into account all the very great problems which we had to face throughout the period covered by the report. (**40**)

6. This is a beautiful place for travellers to stay for a holiday or to enjoy as a stop-over on their way to other resorts. If you plan to visit, you should make a booking as soon as possible. (**38**)

7. All personal property should be covered by insurance of some kind. The cost of replacement is too much for anyone to have to pay themselves, and it is possible to get full cover at a reasonable price these days. (**39**)

8. The officials were very helpful to everyone, all the travel documents were examined speedily, and we were soon on our way to the United States. (**25**)

READING AND WRITING PRACTICE (Contd.)

9.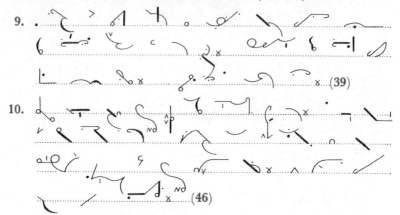

10. (46)

Key to Reading and Writing Practice (Contd.)

9. The approval of the head of your department is necessary before we can make this agreement final with your establishment. As soon as we know that he has agreed we shall take immediate steps. He is an influential man. (39)

10. It is possible to grow beautiful flowers outside in this country throughout the year. A good book on the subject can be very helpful in enabling you to be successful each month with the flowers you like best. How lucky we are to have our gardens. (46)

SHORT FORM AND PHRASE DRILL

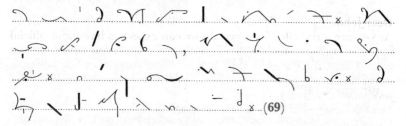

(69)

Key to Short Form and Phrase Drill

From now on there is very little we can do to help you and your company. There will be no more than one large loan this year, and that will be only for a very special reason. You ought to do something about your company before it is too late. There is so much to be done and we think it is up to you to act at once. (69)

ADDITIONAL READING AND WRITING PRACTICE

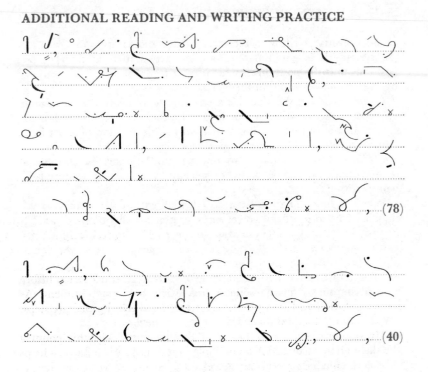

(78)

(40)

Key to Additional Reading and Writing Practice

Dear John,
As you are a traveller I am certain we can expect to have your official approval and personal backing for the new novel out this month, a copy of which I am enclosing. It is a beautiful book with a powerful story. As soon as you have read it, and had time to reflect on it, I feel sure you will agree to support it.
Your assistance would be most influential in increasing sales.
Yours sincerely, (**78**)

Dear Martin,
Thank you for your note. My travels have taken me far and wide but I have not enjoyed a traveller's tale so much for many years. I am happy to support this new book.
Best wishes,
Yours sincerely, (**40**)

THE OMISSION OF VOWELS

Correct position writing in Pitman 2000 is a most important feature of the system. It is essential that outlines are written in their correct positions and the position in which to write an outline is determined by the first vowel sound in the word.

In your study of shorthand it is essential to know all the vowel signs and the correct position in which to write them in an outline. For this reason all the outlines in this book, with the exception of short forms and some phrases, have the vowel signs included. You will by now appreciate, however, that many outlines can be easily recognized and read without any vowel signs, or perhaps with just an essential one being written.

When taking dictation at a speed well within your control, you should place most of the vowel signs. When the dictation is found to be fast, insert only a few essential vowels such as initial or final ones. With experience you will know which outlines need a vowel sign to aid rapid transcription. In general, you will find that long outlines are quite distinctive and do not need vowels at all. Short outlines, with perhaps only one consonant stroke, or a half-length stroke, must have a vowel sign. It is very important to place the diphthongs I, OI, OW, U and the triphones and diphones whenever they occur.

Always complete the consonant strokes for every outline. They are the skeleton of a word. When you have time, or know it to be necessary, add in the further detail—the vowel.

Vowel signs will continue to be shown to help you read quickly. If, when copying or writing from dictation, you feel any are unnecessary, leave them out. If you have difficulty in reading an outline in your notes because there is no vowel sign, you must remember to insert one (or more) the next time you write that outline; but make sure you always write each outline in its correct position.

Now, read all this again. It is **the key to your success.**

UNIT 17
F and V hook
Figures

A **small** hook written at the **end** of a straight stroke, on the circle S side, adds the sound of **F** or **V** in the middle or at the end of a word:

above   advance   advances   advanced   behalf   provide   provided

profit   profited   advantage   advantages   advantageous   forgive

represent   represented   representative   definite   definitely

prefect   prefects   defective   devote   devoted   defence   defences

defensive   defenceless   defend   defends   positive   positively

private   privately   observe   brief   rough   cough   cave

Read the outlines and then write them several times.

At the end of an outline **circle S** is **always** written inside the **F** or **V** hook:

serve	serves	deserve	deserves	prove	proves	give	gives	reserve

reserves	relative	relatives	half	halves	achieve	achieves

A finally hooked thin or thick stroke may be halved for **T** or **D**:

gift	gifts	gifted	draft	drafts	drafted	rift	drift	drifted

The **F** or **V** hook is **not** used when a vowel follows **F** or **V** at the end of a word:

cough **but** coffee   heave **but** heavy   tough **but** toffee

Read the outlines and then write them several times.

FIGURES

Figures 0 to 10, except 0, 2 and 8, and round numbers, are best written as shorthand outlines in continuous matter:

0	2					8				
1	3	4	5	6	7	9	10	20	30	40

All other numbers are represented by Arabic numerals.

Use stroke **N** for hundred: 500   **Th** for thousand: 3,000   **but** £7,000

and **M** for million: 2,900,000 tons/tonnes.

Times of day: (1800 hours), (7 a.m.), (5 p.m.).

Short Forms and Derivatives

difficult   difficulty   thankful

Phrases

The **F** and **V** hook is used to represent the words **of, off,** or **have** in phrases:

part of   type of   lack of   number of   out of   rate of   sort of

in spite of   member of   instead of   city of   range of   better off

you have   who have   who have not   which have   which have not

Tick **the** can be added to the **F** or **V** hook:

part of the   in spite of the   instead of the

PRACTICE PLAN

1. Read through the exercise, referring to the key if necessary.
2. Practise writing any outline which caused any hesitancy in reading.
3. Write each sentence from dictation until you can write it easily and rapidly.
4. Read the sentences from your own shorthand notes.
5. Transcribe the sentences from your own shorthand notes.

READING AND WRITING PRACTICE

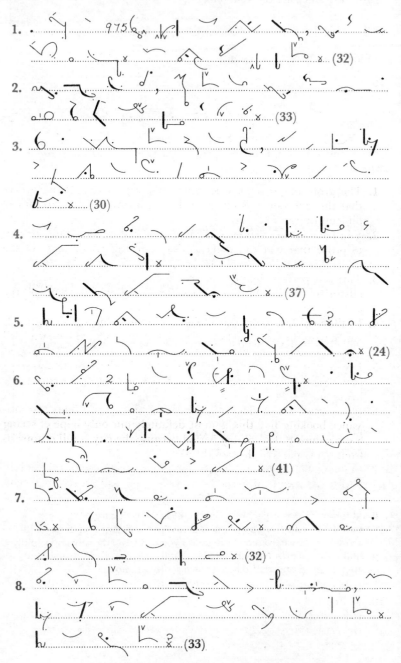

1. .... 975 .... (32)

2. .... (33)

3. .... (30)

4. .... (37)

5. .... (24)

6. .... (41)

7. .... (32)

8. .... (33)

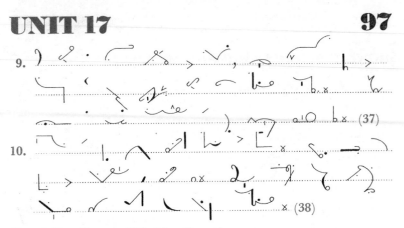

9. ... (37)

10. ... (38)

Key to Reading and Writing Practice

1. The profit of £975,000 outlined in the report before you, proves that the new policy is effective. I am hopeful that we are out of difficult times. (**32**)

2. You have been given every chance, and I think it is time for you to prove that you can make a success of this job in spite of the difficulties that lie ahead. (**33**)

3. This is a perfect time of the year for travel, and we should take advantage of the cheaper rates for flying which some of the airlines are offering just now. (**30**)

4. In the next half year we should be able to achieve a definite advance with the work we have planned. A number of new ideas will have to be investigated before the work can be made final. (**37**)

5. Do you have much hope of receiving any dividends from this company? You deserve some return on your money because profits are being made. (**24**)

6. Please reserve two tickets for either Thursday or Friday. An advance booking like this is most definitely our only hope of seeing a show during the holiday period because the city is full of tourists from many parts of the world. (**41**)

7. On your behalf I have sent a sum of money to the hospital fund. This type of appeal deserves support. You will be sent a receipt for your gift in due course. (**32**)

8. Half of my time is given up to the study of economics, and I am definitely enjoying my work in spite of the pressure felt at times. Do you have any spare time? (**33**)

9. There was a lack of response to the appeal, most likely due to the fact that people usually want more advance notice. I think you should make a new announcement and see how much success it has. (**37**)

10. Coffee and tea will be served at the end of the talk. Please give your ticket to the person who serves you. There is no extra charge for this refreshment because you will already have paid in advance. (**38**)

SHORT FORM AND PHRASE DRILL

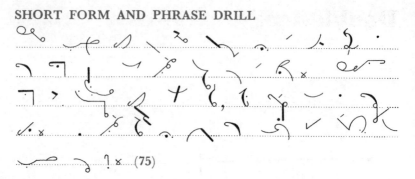

Key to Short Form and Phrase Drill

As soon as possible next month we shall put all the particulars before the meeting and show that there is not a very great difference in the results for this year and last year. As soon as we can get all the facts we shall be able to enlarge on this, and then proceed in a very satisfactory way. The result of this meeting will be very influential on our policy for next year's trading. (**75**)

ADDITIONAL READING AND WRITING PRACTICE

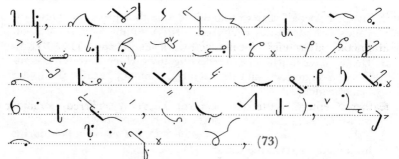

Key to Additional Reading and Writing Practice

Dear David,
You will have observed that the profits for the year are down to almost half of the figures achieved last year in spite of the increased sales. Such results deserve some sort of defence by the Board, and yet nothing has been said on their behalf. This is a difficult problem and, if you have not already done so, I ask you to join me in drafting a protest.
Yours sincerely, (**73**)

UNIT 18
Double-length strokes

Curved strokes are **doubled** in length to represent the sounds of **TER, DER, ThER, THER** and **TURE**. **Circle S** may be added to these double-length strokes:

matter   matters   material   metre   another   sender   after

afternoon   afternoons   future   letter   leader   litres   later   leather

feather   enter   entered   centre   order   ordered   mother

flatter   interrupt   signature   remainder   reminder   Easter   interview

under   understanding   understood   premature   internal

Doubling must not be used when there is a final vowel:

feathery   flattery

Read the outlines and then write them several times.

Straight strokes are **doubled** in length to represent the sounds of **TER, DER, ThER, THER** and **TURE** when they follow another stroke, or have a final hook:

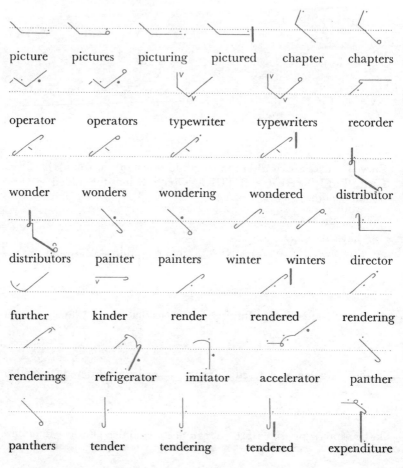

picture	pictures	picturing	pictured	chapter	chapters

operator	operators	typewriter	typewriters	recorder

wonder	wonders	wondering	wondered	distributor

distributors	painter	painters	winter	winters	director

further	kinder	render	rendered	rendering

renderings	refrigerator	imitator	accelerator	panther

panthers	tender	tendering	tendered	expenditure

A straight stroke is **not** doubled if the doubling would produce two strokes of unequal length without an angle:

factor navigator victor

Read the outlines and then write them several times.

Short Forms

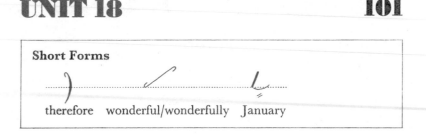

therefore   wonderful/wonderfully   January

Phrases

A stroke may be doubled for the addition of **there/their** or **other**:

I have been   I have been there   I know   I know there is

we know   we know there is   I can be   I can be there   I will be

I will be there   if there   if there is   if there is no   I think there is

some other way   in other ways   my order   your order

their order   my letter   in my letter   your letter

in your letter   for your letter   their letter   later than the

Note that **for there/their** is always written x

PRACTICE PLAN

1. Read through the exercise, referring to the key if necessary.
2. Practise writing any outline which caused any hesitancy in reading.
3. Write each sentence from dictation until you can write it easily and rapidly.
4. Read the sentences from your own shorthand notes.
5. Transcribe the exercise from your own shorthand notes.

READING AND WRITING PRACTICE

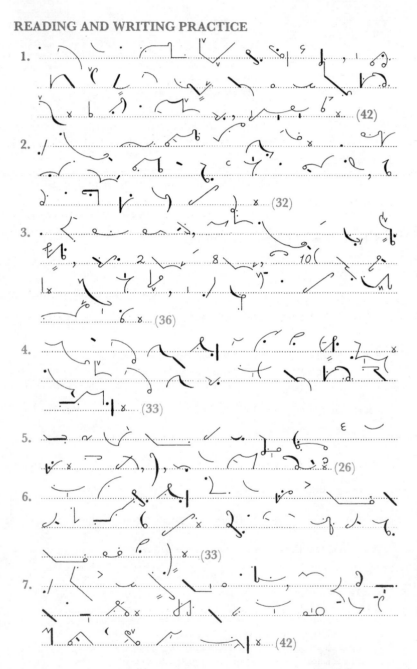

8.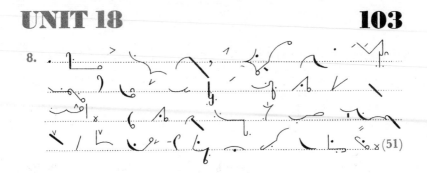

(51)

Key to Reading and Writing Practice

1. An order for an electric typewriter has been placed with the distributor, but he says it will be either January or February before his new deliveries arrive. It is rather a long time to wait, but we know there is no choice. (**42**)

2. Each afternoon many hundreds of letters leave the office. The central mailing room handles all of these with only a small staff, and this says a great deal for their wonderful system. (**32**)

3. The shopping centre is now open, and in the afternoons and evenings on Fridays and Saturdays, between 2 p.m. and 8 p.m., more than ten thousand people use it. I have been there only twice, but on each visit I saw a wonderful variety of materials on sale. (**36**)

4. In future all orders will have to be received not later than the last Thursday of each month. After that time orders will have to wait another month before deliveries can be guaranteed. (**33**)

5. To give you the full picture we need to discuss these matters with you in detail. Can we arrange, therefore, to meet for lunch very soon? (**26**)

6. Another letter has been received asking for details of the pictures to be shown at the gallery this winter. There has been a lot of interest shown in these pictures since last Easter. (**33**)

7. Each chapter of the new Panther book is an adventure, and I am sure there is going to be a good response. It is certain to be yet another success for the author and I do hope that supplies are not interrupted. (**42**)

8. The directors of the firm will be there, and the shareholders will have an opportunity to express their views on the new dividend and interest rates which are to be announced. These rates will not be effective until next November by which time various other changes may well have taken place. (**51**)

READING AND WRITING PRACTICE (Contd.)

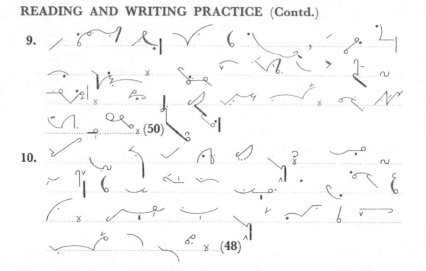

9.

10.

Key to Reading and Writing Practice (Contd.)

9. Our sales manager received your letter this afternoon, and he has asked me to deal with the matter. Please accept my apologies for all the trouble you have experienced. As the main distributors we shall be pleased to renew the material. Simply return the faulty goods as soon as possible. **(50)**

10. I wonder if you have heard of our latest washing powder? In case you have not tried this new product I am enclosing a free sample with this letter. We know there is not another powder on the market which is kinder to materials or to your hands. **(48)**

SHORT FORM AND PHRASE DRILL

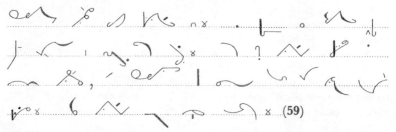

Key to Short Form and Phrase Drill

As soon as we have the results we shall telephone you. The difficulty is that we have been out of touch too long but you have been very patient. Your trading report deserves an immediate response, and as soon as we can do something for you I will let you have full details. This report could be most influential. (59)

ADDITIONAL READING AND WRITING PRACTICE

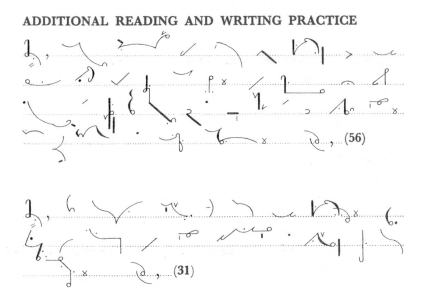

Key to Additional Reading and Writing Practice

Dear Sir,
In future all the materials we order should be delivered to the new centre rather than to our distributor in the city. Our directors met yesterday afternoon and decided that this would be a good idea and would reduce costs. I am sure that you will have an interest in this matter.
Yours faithfully, (56)

Dear Sir,
Thank you for your letter notifying us of your new delivery arrangements. These changes will affect our costs and we enclose a revised tender for your acceptance.
Yours faithfully, (31)

UNIT 19
Shun hook
Negative words
Suffix -ship

A **large** hook written **inside** curves adds the sound of **SHUN**, in the middle or at the end of a word. **Circle S** is written inside the **SHUN** hook:

nation   nations   national   attention   examination   examinations

extension   extensions   explanation   explanations   division   divisions

divisional   relation   relations   fashion   fashions

international   profession   professional   mention   mentions

mentioning   mentioned   pension   pensions   lotion   lotions

solution   solutions   omission   motion   mission   television

Read the outlines and then write them several times.

Words ending in **-able** are generally written with the hooked stroke, but after the **SHUN** hook it is necessary to write, or to disjoin as in:

pensionable   mentionable   fashionable

When a straight stroke has a circle or hook written at the beginning or in the middle of an outline, the **SHUN** hook is written on the opposite side to the circle or hook to balance the outline:

section   sections   collection   collections   exception   exceptions

probation   situation   situations   instruction   inscription

Where there is no circle or hook at the beginning of a straight stroke, the **SHUN** hook is written on the opposite side to the **last** vowel:

operation   co-operation   direction   portion   action

dedication   occasion   education   educational   ration   rational

The **SHUN** hook is **always** written on the right-hand side of simple **T, D** or **J**:

addition   additional   additionally   optician   beautician   magician

Read the outlines and then write them several times.

Sometimes it is necessary to write the **SHUN** hook on the **same** side as the beginning circle or hook to join another stroke to **SHUN**:

station   **but**   stationer stationery stationary

After **F-K, V-K, F-G, V-G, L-K** or **L-G** the **SHUN** hook is written away from the curve, to balance the outline:

election	elections	selection	selections	location	locations

fiction	vocation	vocational	affection	affectionate

Read the outlines and then write them several times.

When the sound of **SHUN** follows the **S, Z,** or **NS, NZ** circle it is represented by a **small** hook written opposite the circle. This hook is written by continuing from the circle on the other side of the stroke. Note the **insertion** of **third** position vowels after **SHUN** but the **omission** of **second** position vowels.

position	positioned	positions	decision	decisions	taxation

transition	transitional	physician	physicians	organization

association	procession	possession	musician	succession

Read the outlines and then write them several times.

NEGATIVE WORDS

Some negative words are formed by prefixing the root word with the strokes **N, L, downward R** or **M**:

necessary	unnecessary	legal	illegal	resolute	irresolute

movable	immovable

UNIT 19 109

In other cases negative words are written:

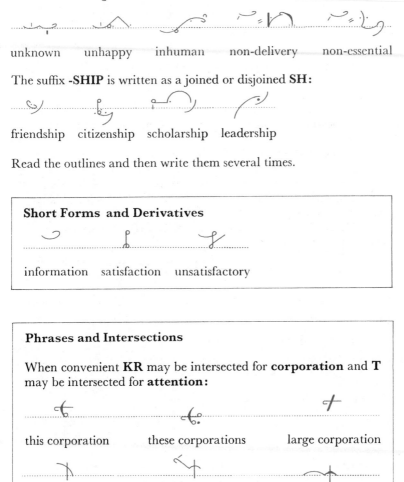

unknown   unhappy   inhuman   non-delivery   non-essential

The suffix **-SHIP** is written as a joined or disjoined **SH**:

friendship   citizenship   scholarship   leadership

Read the outlines and then write them several times.

Short Forms and Derivatives

information   satisfaction   unsatisfactory

Phrases and Intersections

When convenient **KR** may be intersected for **corporation** and **T** may be intersected for **attention**:

this corporation   these corporations   large corporation

your attention   prompt attention   immediate attention

PRACTICE PLAN

1. Read through the exercise beginning on the next page, referring to the key if necessary.
2. Practise writing any outline which caused any hesitancy in reading.
3. Write each sentence from dictation until you can write it easily and rapidly.
4. Read the sentences from your own shorthand notes.
5. Transcribe the exercise from your own shorthand notes.

READING AND WRITING PRACTICE

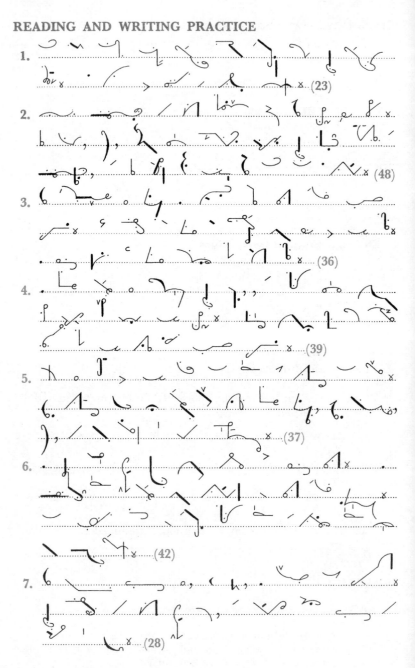

1. .... (23)

2. .... (48)

3. .... (36)

4. .... (39)

5. .... (37)

6. .... (42)

7. .... (28)

8.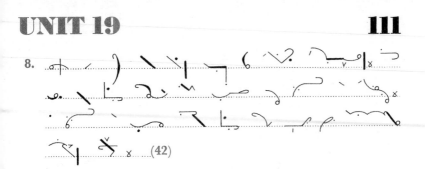

(42)

Key to Reading and Writing Practice

1. Information about entry into the professions can be obtained from the different professional associations. A letter to the secretary should receive immediate attention. (**23**)

2. Many examinations are held at the same time of the year and this situation is not satisfactory. It is felt, therefore, that there should be some co-operation between the different education authorities and examination departments, and it is suggested that they include all this information in a report. (**48**)

3. This organization is changing the location of its head office next week. With the exception of cheques all correspondence should be sent to the new address. The section dealing with cheques remains at the old address. (**36**)

4. The taxation position is very much different today, and additional sums will have to be set to one side to meet the new situation. Deductions will be made direct from employees' salaries at the new rates starting next week. (**39**)

5. Your attention is drawn to the new fashions in stock and the reductions in price. These reductions have been made possible by the latest taxation changes, and these benefits, therefore, are being passed on to our customers. (**37**)

6. The distribution of goods throughout the division will be the responsibility of the section head. The exact stock position should be reported to head office each month. Any necessary action to obtain additional stock and replacement stock must be given prompt attention. (**42**)

7. This picture collection is, without doubt, the finest in the world. Different exhibitions are held throughout the year, and portions of the main collection are always on view. (**28**)

8. Some attention should therefore be paid to getting this operation organized. Action needs to be taken very soon about next year's election of officers. A selection of names can be taken from the current list of members employed by the corporation. (**42**)

READING AND WRITING PRACTICE (Contd.)

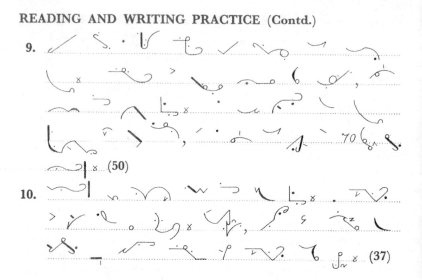

9.

10.

Key to Reading and Writing Practice (Contd.)

9. We are planning an additional extension to our premises in the near future. Expansion of the business makes this necessary, and some immediate action will be taken. A new location for future development might be the answer, and a sum in the region of £70,000 has been mentioned. (50)

10. I mentioned to you earlier about the action I have taken. The co-operation of the whole staff is essential. Fortunately, relations with the employees have always been good and we can expect such co-operation in this situation. (37)

SHORT FORM AND PHRASE DRILL

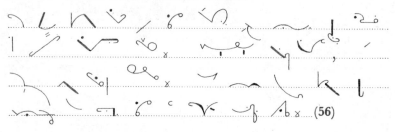

Key to Short Form and Phrase Drill

From January it will be part of our sales policy to offer many different articles at wonderful bargain prices. I know there is no better value, and your order should be placed as soon as possible. In the immediate future it will not be difficult to make arrangements for credit sales with very low interest rates. (56)

ADDITIONAL READING AND WRITING PRACTICE

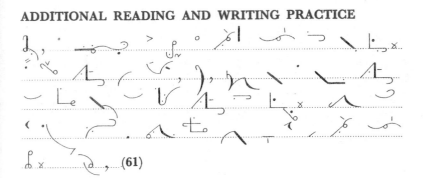

(61)

Key to Additional Reading and Writing Practice

Dear Sir,
An examination of the situation has resulted in some action being taken. A price reduction will follow, therefore, but there will have to be a big reduction in taxation before any additional reduction can take place. We have information that after the election the heavy corporation tax will be cut and that should result in some satisfaction.
Yours faithfully, (61)

UNIT 20
KW, GW, WH

A large hook added to **K** and **G** represents the sounds of **KW** and **GW**. **Circle S** is written inside the hook:

quick	quickly	quicker	quickest	quality	qualities

qualify	qualifies	qualified	qualification	quantity

quarter	distinguish	equal	equally	equalize	equalled

question	questions	questioning	questioned

quite	quiet	quietly	liquid	liquids

require	requires	requiring	requirement	required

request	requests	requesting	requested	square

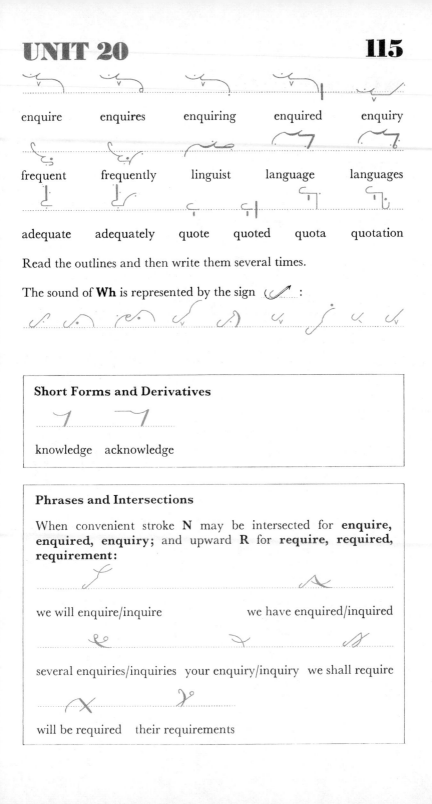

enquire   enquires   enquiring   enquired   enquiry

frequent   frequently   linguist   language   languages

adequate   adequately   quote   quoted   quota   quotation

Read the outlines and then write them several times.

The sound of **Wh** is represented by the sign :

Short Forms and Derivatives

knowledge   acknowledge

Phrases and Intersections

When convenient stroke **N** may be intersected for **enquire, enquired, enquiry;** and upward **R** for **require, required, requirement:**

we will enquire/inquire   we have enquired/inquired

several enquiries/inquiries   your enquiry/inquiry   we shall require

will be required   their requirements

PRACTICE PLAN

1. Read through the exercise, referring to the key if necessary.
2. Practise writing any outline which caused any hesitancy in reading.
3. Write each sentence from dictation until you can write it easily and rapidly.
4. Read the sentences from your own shorthand notes.
5. Transcribe the exercise from your own shorthand notes.

READING AND WRITING PRACTICE

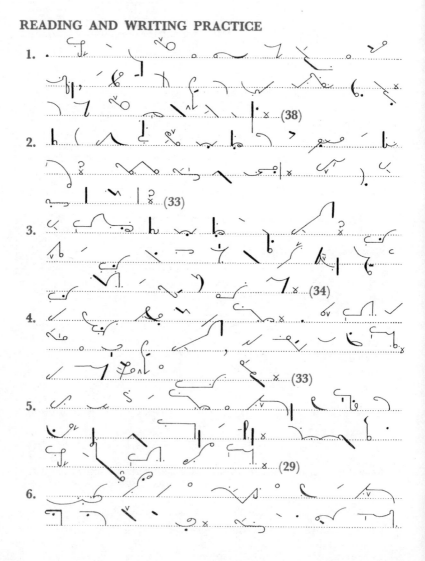

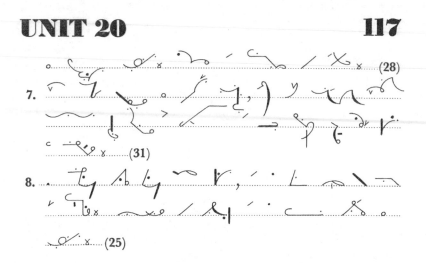

7. ......(31)

8. ......(25)

Key to Reading and Writing Practice

1. The question of food prices is something in which the public is always interested, and this requires your attention throughout the year if you are to represent these people. Your knowledge of prices must be up to date. (**38**)

2. Do you think we have adequate supplies to meet the demands from all the recent enquiries and definite orders? Perhaps production should be increased. Why not see what you can do about it? (**33**)

3. What qualifications do you have to meet the demands of today's world? Equal rights and equal pay can only be really justified for those with equal ability and proof of their skill and knowledge. (**34**)

4. We frequently receive enquiries about our equipment. The high quality of our products is known throughout the world, and we export in vast quantities. We acknowledge all such enquiries as quickly as possible. (**33**)

5. When new plant and equipment is required several quotations from various distributors should be collected and studied. Remember that it is a question of quality as well as quantity. (**29**)

6. International relations are as important as ever and require great care by all nations. Protection of a small country is frequently necessary. Arms and equipment are often required. (**28**)

7. My knowledge of the business is really inadequate, and therefore I shall involve myself in many different aspects of the work and give special attention to those areas dealing with exports. (**31**)

8. The exchange rates change almost daily, and a check must be kept on the quotations. Many enquiries are received and a quick response is necessary. (**25**)

READING AND WRITING PRACTICE (Contd.)

9.
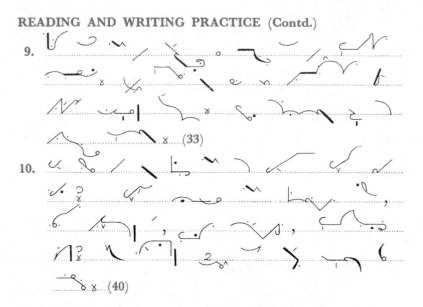

10.

Key to Reading and Writing Practice (Contd.)

9. Additional information about our publications is given in our quarterly magazine. If you require copies to be sent to you regularly just return the enclosed form. Please remember to quote your reference number. (**33**)

10. What steps are to be taken about your work while you are away? Why not make enquiries about temporary staff, salary required and, equally important, qualifications held? I have allocated £200 in the budget to cover this expense. (**40**)

SHORT FORM AND PHRASE DRILL

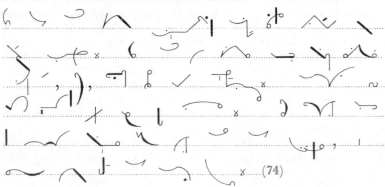

(74)

Key to Short Form and Phrase Drill

Thank you for the information which will be incorporated into the sales department report to be published next month. This information will help us to give better service and, therefore, greater satisfaction to our customers. In your letter you have also called our attention to several difficult matters. There is very little I can do immediately because I have little influence in the finance department, but something will be done in the near future. (**74**)

ADDITIONAL READING AND WRITING PRACTICE

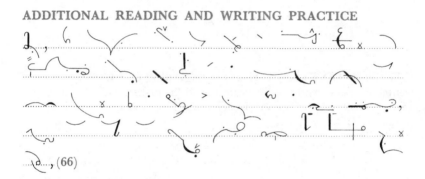

...(66)

Key to Additional Reading and Writing Practice

Dear Sir,

Thank you for your letter applying for the position of accountant with this company. Your qualifications appear to be adequate and an interview will be arranged in the immediate future. It is a special requirement of the firm that you have a medical examination, and if you have any knowledge of any previous illnesses you must draw the doctor's attention to them.

Yours faithfully, (**66**)

UNIT 21
Dot CON, COM
Disjoining for
CON, COM, CUM, COG
Disjoined half-length T

The sounds **CON** and **COM** at the **beginning** of a word are represented by a dot written at the beginning of the first stroke in the outline.
The position of the outline is determined by the first vowel sound
following **CON** or **COM**:

condition   control   contract   continue   continues   continuous

contact   consider   considerable   considerably   connect   connection

confirmation   concern   concerns   confer   conference   conferences

common   commonly   company   completed   completion   comment

convenient   constant   contain   contains   contribute   consequence

Read the outlines and then write them several times.

In the **middle** of a word the sound of **CON, COM, CUM** or **COG** is represented by writing the stroke following any of these sounds close to the preceding stroke and omitting the dot:

discontinue   reconsider   reconsiders   reconsidering   disconnect

disconnecting   disconnected   self-control   self-controlled

self-contained   self-confident   incomplete   uncommon   uncommonly

recommend   recommendation   uncomfortable   circumstances

recognize   recognition

Read the outlines and then write them several times.

In order to avoid the joining together of strokes of unequal length, and in outlines containing a series of T's, a disjoined **half-length T** following **stroke T** is used:

attitude   substitute   institute   destitute

Short Forms

nevertheless   notwithstanding

Phrases

In phrases the dot **CON** or **COM** is omitted and the sound of **CON** or **COM** is expressed by writing outlines close together:

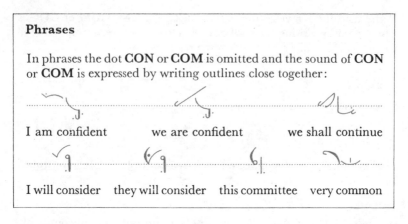

I am confident   we are confident   we shall continue

I will consider   they will consider   this committee   very common

PRACTICE PLAN

1. Read through the exercise, referring to the key if necessary.
2. Practise writing any outline which caused any hesitancy in reading.
3. Write each sentence from dictation until you can write it easily and rapidly.
4. Read the sentences from your own shorthand notes.
5. Transcribe the exercise from your own shorthand notes.

READING AND WRITING PRACTICE

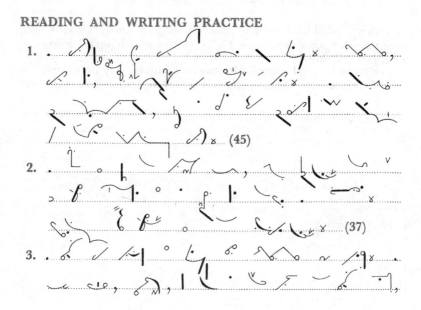

1. ... (45)

2. ... (37)

3. ...

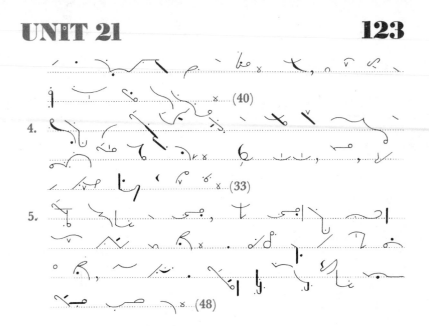

4.

5.

Key to Reading and Writing Practice

1. The weather conditions throughout the world seem to be changing. Perhaps, one day, scientists will be able to control our sunshine and rain. The benefits would be remarkable, but there is a chance that we would be concerned about the boredom which follows perfect weather. **(45)**

2. The contract is due for renewal now, and if it would be convenient for you I would suggest Monday as a suitable day for completing the agreement. Please confirm that this suggestion is in every way convenient. **(37)**

3. The hotel we recommended has changed hands and perhaps you should reconsider. The new owners, however, do have a fine record in hotel catering, and a remarkable list of achievements. Nevertheless, you might want to consider another place for your conference. **(40)**

4. Severe competition will probably follow the opening of any business by manufacturers of similar products in this area. This is not uncommon, of course, but we should recognize the danger that lies ahead. **(33)**

5. Company profits for the year continue to increase, notwithstanding the increased competition mentioned in my report to you last year. The circumstances today are much the same as last year, and in recommending the proposed dividend I am confident that we shall continue to make progress next year. **(48)**

READING AND WRITING PRACTICE (Contd.)

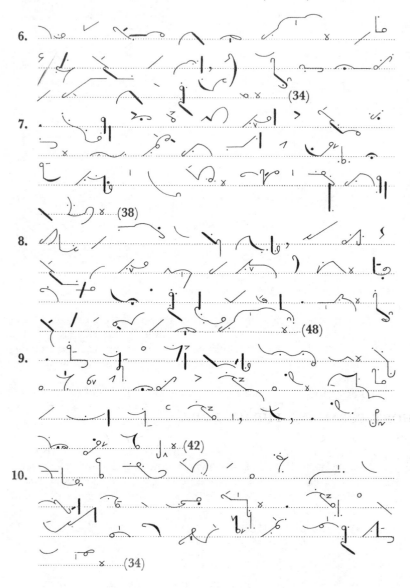

6.

(34)

7.

(38)

8.

(48)

9.

(42)

10.

(34)

Key to Reading and Writing Practice (Contd.)

6. Your comments on our programmes will be most welcome. Our contacts with the general public are limited, and therefore any contribution you can make concerning our work will be of considerable value to us. (**34**)

7. The conference considered all the main points and also recognized all the problems awaiting action. Many resolutions were carried and the various committees made strong recommendations on future policies. More controls on expenditure were considered to be essential. (**38**)

8. We shall continue our campaign for better living conditions, and we are certain that the public will recognize how much we require their help. Donations from large companies have made a considerable difference to our funds during the current year. Contributions both large and small are most welcome. (**48**)

9. The construction industry has enjoyed boom conditions for many years now. Competition is only slight and the main concern of the employer is staff. Long-term contracts are entered into with employees but, nevertheless, the staffing situation remains serious in this town. (**42**)

10. Your company continues with its expansion policy and is constantly looking for improved methods to increase productivity. The employees' committee has put forward some very useful ideas resulting in some considerable reduction in costs. (**34**)

SHORT FORM AND PHRASE DRILL

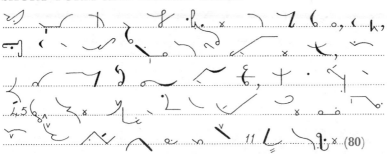

(80)

Key to Short Form and Phrase Drill

I wish to call your attention to this unsatisfactory state of affairs. Your knowledge of this is, without doubt, greater than that of anyone because of your particular work. Nevertheless, I am sure you will acknowledge that there is something wrong with this company, notwithstanding a profit of £45,000 for the year. I shall continue to ask for further information. Six copies of my final report will be sent to you by 11 January for your consideration. (**80**)

ADDITIONAL READING AND WRITING PRACTICE

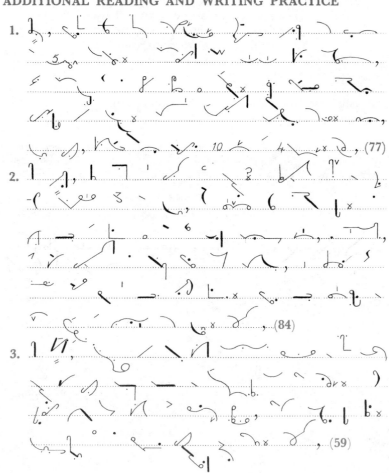

1. ... (77)

2. ... (84)

3. ... (59)

ADDITIONAL READING AND WRITING PRACTICE
(Contd.)

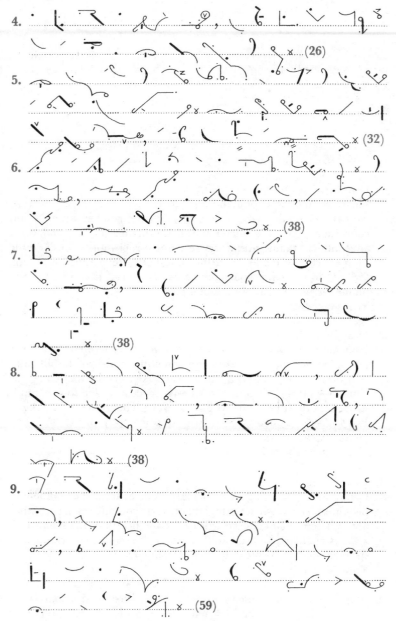

4. .... (26)

5. .... (32)

6. .... (38)

7. .... (38)

8. .... (38)

9. .... (59)

10.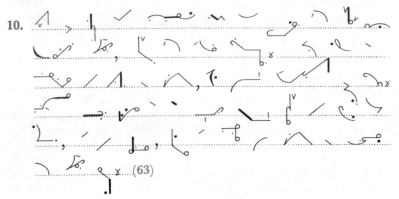

....(63)

Key to Additional Reading and Writing Practice

1. Dear Sir,
   Please contact this company at your earliest convenience so that
   we can reconsider your claim of £500 for compensation. I am
   concerned about the uncommon delay in this matter, and yet I
   am confident that a satisfactory settlement is possible. Considerable
   progress can be made when the conditions are favourable. I look
   forward to receiving your comments. You may, if you wish, telephone me between 10 a.m. and 4 p.m.
   Yours faithfully, (**77**)

2. Dear Reader,
   Do you get on well with people? It is worth trying to see the other
   person's point of view, although sometimes this can be difficult.
   A little give and take is all that is needed to make the home, the
   country, and the whole world a better place in which to live, but it
   seems that the accent always has to be on giving rather than taking.
   Please give some consideration to my philosophy and let me know
   your views.
   Yours sincerely, (**84**)

3. Dear George,
   Conferences are being held in many centres to attract influential
   people who will wish to get together to form committees in particular
   areas. Their chief concern will be for the health of the senior citi-
   zens, particularly in these difficult days. If you can contribute as a
   speaker we shall be pleased to hear from you.
   Yours sincerely, (**59**)

4. A debate can be a useful exercise, if all those taking part in it
   consider the points for and against the motion before preparing
   their speeches. (**26**)

Key to Additional Reading and Writing Practice (Contd.)

5. Most firms offer their employees facilities to enjoy their favourite sports and hobbies after working hours. Many splendid sports grounds are owned by business organizations, and others have Drama and Music groups. (**32**)

6. Railways and roads are at the heart of a country's transport system. Their maintenance, and in the case of the railways the services they offer, are a necessary part of the economic stability and growth of the nation. (**38**)

7. Education is not merely a matter of learning strings of facts and passing examinations, although these are part of life. Someone once said that true education is what remains when you have forgotten everything you have been taught. (**38**)

8. It is good to spend your spare time doing something you like, whether it be playing football or hockey, making your own clothes, or becoming a potter. Such activities can be more rewarding than watching too much television. (**38**)

9. Much can be achieved in a meeting if the agenda has been planned with care, and if the chairman is firm and fair. The work of the secretary, who is writing the minutes, is also helped if the meeting is conducted in an orderly fashion. This applies equally to the business meeting and to that of the social committee. (**59**)

10. Write to the editor of our magazine about any queries or ideas you may have concerning shorthand, typing or office practice. Her staff of experts are ready to help, and they look forward to hearing from you. Catalogues giving details of all current book titles are free for the asking, and our discs, tapes and cassettes will help to increase your shorthand speed. (**63**)

SHORT FORMS

Examples of **some** common derivatives are shown indented

a/an		first	
able to		for	
accord/according/		from	
according to		gentleman	
accordingly		gentlemen	
all		had/dollar	
almost		have	
although		having[1]	
always		he (phrasing only)	
also		how	
altogether		I/eye	
and		immediate	
any/in		immediately	
anybody		influence	
anyhow		influenced[1]	
anyone		influencing[1]	
anything		influential	
are		information	
as/has		is/his	
be		it	
being[1]		January	
before		knowledge	
but		acknowledge	
cannot		large	
commercial/ly		largely	
could		larger	
dear		largest	
difficult		manufacture	
difficulty		manufactured[1]	
do		manufacturer	
enlarge		manufactures	
enlarged[1]		manufacturing[1]	
enlargement		more	
enlarger		nevertheless	
enlarging[1]		notwithstanding	

of		the (tick used in	
on		phrasing)	
ought		there/their	
our/hour		therefore	
ours/hours		thing	
ourselves		anything	
owe/oh		nothing	
owed[1]		something	
owes		think	
owing[1]		thinking[1]	
particular		this	
particularly		to/too[2]	
particulars		today[3]	
put		to be	
puts		together	
putting[1]		trade/toward	
responsible/		towards	
responsibility		very	
satisfaction		we	
satisfactory		which	
several		who	
shall		will	
should		with	
subject		without	
subjected[1]		wonderful/ly	
subjecting[1]		would	
subjects		year	
thank		yesterday	
thanked[1]		you	
thankful		your	
thanking[1]		yours	
thanks		yourself	
that			

[1] Past tenses of short forms conform to the disjoined **T** and **D** rule. For the present participle of short forms dot **ING** is used.

[2] In Pitman 2000 the numeral is used for **two**.

[3] The vowel is included to distinguish **today** from **to do**.

INTERSECTIONS

arrange/arranged/		department		........|........
arrangement	........⌐........	enquire/enquiry/		
attention	........|........	inquire/inquiry		........⌣........
business	........⬎........	form		........⬐........
charge	......../........	month		(
company	........‒........	require/required/		
company limited	........⌒........	requirement		......../........
corporation	........⊂........			

Circle S may be added to intersections to indicate plurals or possessive case.